Ancient Egyptian Magic

The Ultimate Guide to Gods, Goddesses, Divination, Amulets, Rituals, and Spells of Ancient Egypt

Your Free Gift
(only available for a limited time)

Thanks for getting this book! If you want to learn more about various spirituality topics, then join Mari Silva's community and get a free guided meditation MP3 for awakening your third eye. This guided meditation mp3 is designed to open and strengthen ones third eye so you can experience a higher state of consciousness. Simply visit the link below the image to get started.

https://spiritualityspot.com/meditation

Table of Contents

Introduction

Have you ever wondered about the ancient Egyptian religion? Perhaps you have wondered what deities they worshiped and what sort of magic they practiced.

Even though ancient Egyptian religion and magic may seem like relics of a bygone era, they have fascinated people for generations and still do to this day. Numerous hermetic orders have incorporated Egyptian magic and religion into their practices. Orders such as the Rosicrucian Order, Hermetic Order of the Golden Dawn, and Stella Matutina incorporated many Egyptian beliefs into their practices, such as the use of the ankh and nemes headdress.

However, it's also true that the ancient Egyptian religion has become diluted and distorted over the years, so much so that it can be challenging to tell which traditions are real and which were added by later practitioners.

This book will help you to understand ancient Egyptian religion and magic in greater detail. It's an excellent introduction for newcomers interested in ancient Egyptian magic and experienced practitioners looking for further guidance. We'll explore what the ancient Egyptians thought about magic, the deities they worshiped and which were associated with their magical practice, and their beliefs in philosophy, cosmology, and the creation of the universe.

We'll explore the critical importance of magic not only in ancient Egyptian religion and funerary practices but also in their daily life. Many of the symbols we only know today as hieroglyphs had magical significance, and we'll look at some of the most important ones. We'll also look at the vital role that amulets and other magical tools played in Egyptian society.

This book isn't simply a scholarly overview of ancient Egyptian magical practice. We also offer easy and effective ways to incorporate ancient Egyptian magic into your daily life.

This book will help you make your own ancient Egyptian amulets and give you a better understanding of how to use other magical tools like ushabti figures. We'll also cover divination in ancient Egypt and explain how these forms of divination can be used in today's world. Furthermore, we'll look at the use of sacred plants and herbs in ancient Egyptian spell work and show you how you can use them in your magical practice.

Finally, we'll offer an overview of different types of ancient Egyptian spells and rituals. We'll offer a list of spells and rituals you can use as your starting point when incorporating ancient Egyptian magic into your life and provide instructions on how to carry out these rituals. We'll also offer ways to incorporate ancient Egyptian magic with new-age magical practices.

Chapter 1: Ancient Egyptians and Magic

Unlike the modern-day definition of magic, ancient Egyptian magic didn't involve illusions, tricks, or weird hats. Instead, it revolved around the power of the natural laws created by mystical or supernatural figures. According to ancient Egyptian beliefs, creation and existence went hand-in-hand with magic. As you will learn in the following chapter, the creation of the cosmos, the maintenance of peace, and the dynamics of daily life all involved magic. It served as a source of healing and abundance, a method of reassurance, and a guarantee of the afterlife. It touched every aspect of living, from waking up in the morning and engaging in social interactions to preparing or cooking food. Ancient Egyptians believed that their cycle of life was itself magic. Pregnancy, birth, the journey of life, death, and the concept of the afterlife were all governed by a deity who was greater and older than existence. This deity is what we know as Heka or magic.

Ancient Egyptians believed priests, pharaohs, magicians, and even people, could invoke magic through gods and goddesses. The fact that it was a vital part of healing ceremonies and rituals shows just how important magic was. Practitioners used sacred writings and spells to protect themselves against diseases, evil, and any form of danger. While magic was mainly associated with noble purposes, such as healing, protection, and as a supplement to the field of medicine, some people used it for malefic purposes like black magic and casting evil spells and curses. It was also thought that inanimate objects, like amulets and wands, could be infused with magical properties.

Heka, in a nutshell, was the deified form of magic. Some deities like Bes, Shed, Wadjet, and Tutu used it to help and protect humans. For instance, women who struggled to get pregnant were often advised to visit a Bes Chamber in a temple and spend an evening there. Ancient Egyptians thought this practice could help them conceive, which is why these rooms were often called incubation chambers. Bes was the god of fertility, childbirth, and sexuality, which is why infertile women carried the deity's amulets and had tattoos of it.

Bes was also a popular symbol of protection upon childbirth. The family of newborn children often used Bes amulets and images to protect them during childhood. These traditions were taught to them as they entered adulthood. Later, you will learn that magic and rituals were also practiced upon a person's death.

In this chapter, you will learn all about Heka and magic in ancient Egypt. Here, you will learn about the different types of magic and how it was practiced in life and upon death.

What Is Heka?

Heka is the embodiment of magic and medicine as a deity. Deified magic, or Heka, comes before any other deity in the Egyptian pantheon of gods and goddesses. The term itself means "magic" in the ancient Egyptian language. Heka was also used to refer to supernatural entities and forces, especially those who contributed to the creation of the universe and the cosmos. A literal translation of the word "Heka" would be "the usage of ka." According to ancient Egyptian religion, ka is the divine spirit or vital life force that protects an individual. It is a portion or facet of the soul of both deities and individuals. It was thought that the ka continued to live on after the person had died (a little like we think of a soul). Ancient Egyptians thought it resided in statues, icons, or pictures, which is why they built numerous statues of their rulers and deities.

Since Heka could be accessed and practiced by everyone, it could also be used for both noble and malefic purposes. This is why the term can be somewhat understood as a supernatural process to cause a desired outcome or change. Egyptologists suggest that it can also be loosely understood as a system that the ancient Egyptians used to deal with irrational or unjustifiable events and situations. In mythology, the symbol for Heka contains both serpents that Heka once defeated. There are many configurations, but they are usually either above her head or around her raised arms.

To further illustrate the significance of Heka in ancient Egyptian culture, it must be noted that ancient Egyptian physicians named themselves the "priests of Heka." Egyptians usually referred to them for help regarding magic or healing. They also consulted those physicians whenever they sought protection against disease and illnesses. Traditional medical techniques were typically supplemented with magical rites and rituals to heal patients.

You will find that numerous ancient Egyptian pharaohs, gods, and goddesses were portrayed alongside Heka flails or scepters on tablets, scarabs, and statues. Egyptian rulers and individuals of power were pictured carrying a scepter of sekhem, or power. This scepter was used to allocate terrestrial power to its carrier. You may be surprised to learn that Seichim, a modern-day healing technique similar to reiki, is derived from the word "sekhem." This scepter, however, is not to be confused with the Heka scepter, which was designed to delegate magical abilities and powers for healing purposes.

The word Heka refers to the deity and the magical practice itself. In other words, during their Heka practice, practitioners invoked Heka. This deity was first identified during the Predynastic period, and the concept was further elaborated on during the Early Dynastic Period. You will also find it in the ancient texts: Pyramid & Coffin, Intermediate Period, and the Old Kingdom.

Like Maat, the goddess (more on that later), Heka had no temples or cults. This is not because the deity lacked power but simply because the concept of Heka affected every aspect of the life of the average ancient Egyptian. When referring to Maat or Heka, it is usually the underlying concept or force being referred to.

Practitioners and Techniques

As you can probably tell by now, the creator used numerous forces, including magic, to establish the cosmos. According to ancient Egyptian lore, even symbolic behaviors can result in real or tangible outcomes. All gods and goddesses of the Egyptian pantheon were believed to possess this ability. However, their magical powers varied, as did the regulations regarding how each could put Heka into practice.

The reason why experienced priests were the primary practitioners of Heka was that they were believed to be the protectors of confidential and special information that was granted to them by the deities. This knowledge was thought to be a gift to humanity that could alleviate bad fate. Lector priests who could understand ancient magical books were the most highly esteemed practitioners of Heka. These individuals were thought to bring wax animal figures to life. Ancient Egyptians also believed that lector priests could push back the water of lakes. They also performed rituals to protect their rulers and even help reincarnate the dead. The priests who were associated with Sekhmet, the goddess of the plague, were particularly the most talented when it came to healing magic.

Scorpion charmers performed rituals to eliminate the poisonous effects of insects.
https://www.pexels.com/photo/black-and-brown-insect-with-pincers-1981542/

The scorpion charmers came next. As one can tell from the name, these practitioners used magic to eliminate the poisonous effects of insects and reptiles. Midwives, nurses, and other medical professionals were also known to incorporate magic into their practices. Amulets, which ancient Egyptians could obtain from specialized priests, were another popular source of Heka.

Ancient Egyptians mostly practiced magic at dawn. Those practicing would remain pure to enhance the magic, abstaining from sex and romantic relationships. They would also stay away from women who were menstruating and active embalmers. To add to their purity, they would bathe and wash thoroughly, wear clean clothes, and eat clean food before performing any rites.

Written magic was considered the most esteemed form of practice because very few ancient Egyptians were literate. Spells typically comprised both spoken words and physical actions. All the words needed to be pronounced correctly because only then would they activate the magic inside the amulet or the potion.

Types of Magic

As we mentioned above, there were two types of magic; protective, healing, white or benefic magic, and unfortunate, harmful, black, or malefic magic.

Besides healing and protection, white magic was often used to cast love spells, encourage conception and childbirth, accompany the deceased on their journey to the afterlife, and so on. On the other hand, black magic was typically associated with hexes, voodoo, and curses. Most deities who practiced Heka were protective gods and goddesses, meaning they practiced white or healing magic.

Amulets that were charged with white magic were used to fend off evil spirits and attract abundance or other beneficial forces. While black magic could be practiced, it was believed that whoever conducted it would face severe repercussions. Ancient Egyptians believed in the concept of karma and valued the idea of reciprocity.

Magic in Life

Wise women who were known as seers were not only able to foresee the future but also served as healing instruments. Many Egyptologists believe that these individuals were a constant aspect of spiritual belief. Seers could help with the interpretation of visions or dreams, encourage conception and childbirth, and prescribe herbal remedies. Seers were not necessarily literate. However, they, among other individuals, often memorized spells so they could use them whenever they needed to.

Ancient Egyptians of all social classes relied on Heka and magical practices in numerous aspects of their daily lives. Everyone, from rulers and esteemed members of society to enslaved people and peasants, used magic and believed in its power to change situations. Egyptologists have confirmed this information by examining the number of charms and amulets found at historical Egyptian sites. It was a very effective method of self-defense because anyone with just the right amount of knowledge could employ it in their favor. This meant that even when nurses, doctors, 0r priests weren't around, people could still cast their own spells and perform the appropriate rituals.

There were charms and rituals for every purpose. For instance, magic was the answer if someone needed to boost their business or productivity, overcome a challenge, beat an illness, promote fertility, or even curse their adversary. In ancient Egypt, a person's name was related to their identity. In fact, they believed that each person was granted a secret name, which was also known as "the ren." However, this name was only known by the individual and the deities. Finding out what another person's secret name was meant that this individual had been overpowered. However, discovering another person's secret name was not the only way to gain control over them. Slandering them or fully erasing their name from history was another way to do so.

Magic in Death

Heka was just as significant in death as it was in daily life. Mummification, perhaps the most popular ancient Egyptian form of magic, was practiced to preserve the deceased's body. The main idea behind mummification was to ensure that the person's soul would be able to find them in the afterlife. The priests also conducted a final ritual at the deceased's funeral. It was known as the "Opening of the Mouth Ceremony" and involved the usage of objects to touch the corpse in various places. The purpose behind this practice was to ensure that the deceased could utilize all their senses in the afterlife. They also used amulets to protect the mummies in the tomb and left practical and favored objects so they could be utilized in the afterlife.

Even if you practice modern forms of magic, it may feel impossible to wrap your head around the ancient ways of magic. This is because, over time, we've obtained a different and more enhanced understanding of the world around us. No matter how sophisticated ancient Egyptian beliefs appeared to be, they didn't necessarily depict the ultimate truth and secrets of the universe.

Chapter 2: Creation, Cosmology, and Philosophy

The ancient Egyptian myth of creation is very elaborate, like other tales and fables. It is no surprise that there are numerous renditions of the Egyptian tale of how the cosmos came into existence. In essence, it was believed that the gods responsible for the world's creation were the ones who dictated the flow of nature, the societal structures, and the basic principles of life. The myth of creation is found in ancient texts, buildings, scrolls, tombs, and temples. The tale recounts how the god Atum managed to create the Earth out of nothing but chaos. This is why they held the Earth in the highest regard, trusting that it was a sacred place that mirrored the home of the gods in the sky.

According to the ancient Egyptians, the creation of the cosmos was not an overnight job. Instead, they thought the universe was created over extended periods when the gods resided on Earth. Each of them built kingdoms on the foundations of justice and passed it onto the rightful Pharoah when it was time to return to the sky.

The Egyptian Book of the Dead explains that the god of Heliopolis, Atum, was the one behind the creation of the universe. It recounts that the world was nothing but a vast space of darkness and waters that flowed without direction. It was known as "Nun." Nun embodied a total of 4 pairs of both female and male deities. Each pair symbolized one of the 4 Nun principles, which are infinite water, invisibility, darkness, and a diminished sense of direction.

The creation of the universe started when Atum created himself out of nothingness. He used his name's power and will to emerge out of Nun. He was thenceforth known as the creator of all deities and humans and was charged with instilling order on Earth and in the sky (or heavens). Atum was the ruler of the Heavens and Earth, which is why he held the symbol of life known as the ankh. Atum carried a scepter wherever he went, the symbol of authority within the monarchy, and he is depicted with that along with the double crown.

In this chapter, we will uncover the ancient Egyptian myth of creation. We will also delve deep into the ancient Egyptian worldview, spiritual beliefs, and the concept of the afterlife. By the end, you will have grasped an understanding of philosophies like the 7 Maat principles and the idea of heart-weighing before Aaru.

The Ancient Egyptian Myth of Creation

The stories recounted on the walls of the Pyramids suggest that Atum created himself out of darkness and chaos and arose as a Bennu bird. When the sun rose, Atum took flight, traveling from Heliopolis, and landing on an obelisk (Benben) – the representation of the sun's light. He became engulfed in fire after building a nest of branches and herbs. In most pyramids, and with some obelisks, you will see a capstone at the peak. This stone symbolizes rebirth, renewal, and everlasting life.

At the start of creation, Atum created twins, a son and a daughter. The son, Shu, represents the arid air around us, and the daughter, Tefnut, represents the moist air. Together, they represented life and justice, or right, the two universal fundamental principles of human existence. They were also responsible for parting the heavens from the water. Shu and Tefnut became parents, bringing Nut and Geb into the world. Nut represents the sky, and Geb represents the land (dry land). When the primordial waters receded (Nut), an earthy mound was revealed (Geb). This gave way to the first piece of solid dry land where Re, the sun god, was finally able to rest. Atum was referred to as Re during the ancient Egyptian dynastic period. The title Re alluded to the first rising of the sun.

Together, Geb and Nut created four children; the god of order, Osiris, the god of disorder, Seth, and Isis and Nephthys, their sisters. The offspring of Geb and Nut gave way to a whole new generation that finally contributed to the cessation of the Heliopolitan Ennead. This Ennead was made up of nine deities, starting with Atum.

As we mentioned above, the myth of creation is recounted in several ways. One story tells of the Heliopolitan Ennead being replaced with the Ogdoad, utilizing a group of eight gods. The Ogdoad consisted of 4 pairs of male and female deities representing primeval chaos and all its aspects. The gods were portrayed as frogs and the goddesses as snakes. The names of the deities that symbolized water were Nun and Naunet. Amun and Amaunet personified the principle of invisibility or hiddenness. Heh and Huahet combine to represent infinity, while Ket and Kauket represent darkness.

The Eye of Re, the Sun God

The eye of Re depicts the power to see, shed light, and take action.
Polyester,fi:Käyttäjä:kompak, CC BY-SA 3.0 <http://creativecommons.org/licenses/by-sa/3.0/>, via Wikimedia Commons: https://commons.wikimedia.org/wiki/File:Eye_of_Ra.svg

Re, the sun god, governed the Earth. At that period, the land was where both divine bodies and humans existed peacefully. According to mythology, Re's eye was responsible for the creation of humanity. This is why the eye of Re was also known as Wedjat, which means the eye of wholeness. Humankind was born from Re's eye when it became separated from his body. Shu and Tefnut both tried to catch it, but they were unable, and the tears were shed through the struggle, humans forming from those tears.

Atum is often depicted as an eye, the symbol popular with many deities, including Re and Horus (the son of Osiris and Isis). The eye of Re is also a depiction of the power to see, shed light, and take action. Returning the eye to its owner, the creator, would be a symbol of healing for the Earth. It meant that essential constructs such as order and justice would again be restored to the land. Maintaining these principles meant stopping chaos from spreading on Earth. Keeping the peace was an essential role of the Pharaoh.

The alternative version to this story suggests that when the Wedjat decided to leave, Re asked the moon god, Thoth, to bring it back. He went to fetch it only to find that another eye had replaced the one that had wandered off. Normally, the original eye was furious, so Re decided to place it on his brow. However, he shaped it into a cobra goddess known as the uraeus, so it could rule the entire universe. Ever since that happened, the pharaohs placed the symbol of the cobra goddess on their brows to symbolize protection. The placement of the uraeus also showed that they were Re's descendants.

The Outburst of Rebellion

When Re grew older, the deities avidly used his softening brain and growing confusion. It was also believed that humans, too, tried to take advantage of his condition. This caused them to fall out of divine grace. Re, being the great god he was, didn't stay silent in the face of rebellion. He sent his eye out to slaughter those who turned against him. He shapeshifted into Sekhmet, the powerful female deity who took the form of a lioness to punish his adversaries. When he had finished, he transformed into the goddess Hathor who appeared as a cow.

Although he won, Re was worn down by his pain and worries. He decided to flee the world, still taking the shape of Hathor. Hathor ascended to the heavens above, riding atop Nut (the sky). Those deities who clung to Hathor's stomach went with him, and they became the stars in the night sky. The moon watches over us, and that is because Thoth (the moon god) was given magic to protect humans. At this point, the heavens and the mortal realm, people and gods, split.

The Journey of Re

Re took to the skies, birthed each morning to journey from each other to the west. He used a boat (known as the Bark of Millions of Years), and a few other gods also joined him to help. Khepri, the scarab god, carried Re across the sky. Apep, his main enemy, was a huge serpent that resided in the Nile. The Nile River was believed to be the waters of the Nun. Although Apep continuously tried to block the boat's passage, Re always emerged victorious.

As you can tell by now, Re was the most significant deity in the entire pantheon of Egyptian gods. He had numerous names and titles, including Aten, which meant the sun disk, and Khepri, meaning the rising sun. At the sun's height or zenith, he was known as the scarab, and his most popular name, Re, referred to his role as the supreme god of Heliopolis. The deity was also known as Atum at sunset.

Obelisks, the sphinx, and the pyramids all relate closely to Re. When the sun rose, it looked like it was winged, and this winged journeyman (or journey-god) was depicted as Re-Horakhty. At some point in history, this god was symbolized by the sphinx. The scarab also symbolized Re because it buried its eggs in a hole where they hatched like the sun god pushed out the sun from the eastern horizon.

Worldview and Spiritual Beliefs

Ancient Egyptians were polytheistic, which meant that they believed in the existence of several gods. They believed that each deity had unique characteristics and capabilities, as well as a distinct nature. Like other polytheistic religions, the deities of the ancient Egyptians neither had unending power nor limitless knowledge. They were still much more powerful than the average human being and nearly immortal. Ancient Egyptian deities could also normally survive fatal blows or wounds, managed to be present in more than one place at a single time, and could impact people in both visible and invisible ways. Most deities were benevolent. However, one couldn't always count on their favors. This is why people always had to ensure that their deities were appeased and satisfied.

Unfortunately, the traits and characteristics of each deity were not always strictly known. Many of them, however, had primary associations. For instance, Re was linked to the sun, and Hathor was associated with women. It's worth noting that there were a lot of overlapping features between major gods, though. It could also be observed that the deities with more restricted characteristics had the least power. As you may recall, a single god or mythological figure could go by more than one name. The three main social classes of deities were males, females, and younger deities.

Gods were generally associated with certain geographical locations. Heliopolis, Memphis, is the original location of the sun cult, and the cult is related to Ptah, Thebes, and Amon. They also had main manifestations and typically corresponded to at least one animal species. As for the gods, the bull and the falcon were the most significant figures. The female deities were usually associated with lionesses, cows, vultures, and cobras. Some deities, however, had specific associations. Sebek, for example, was linked to the crocodile. Thoth corresponded to two animals; the baboon and the ibis.

Ka, which refers to the vital energy or life force of a human, was transferred from one generation to the following one. The "ba" is the force that enables us to move freely and appear in different forms. This force was mainly associated with the next world. Your "akh" is your spirit once it has left this world for the next.

Gods often took the form of humans. Some of them only showed up in human form (Min and Ptah especially). They would also appear as part human and part animal, taking the head of the animal associated with them. The sphinx is an exception, where the human and animal parts are switched. Sphinxes were also often depicted with other heads, such as that of a falcon or a ram.

The ancient Egyptian religion lasted for over 3000 years. Egyptians were very spiritual, and their religion was incorporated into numerous aspects of their lives. They always aimed to provide for their deities, ensure their satisfaction, and obtain their favor. The ancient Egyptian spiritual beliefs were very intricate and complex. This intricacy could be observed through the various manifestations of the deities and the numerous mythological roles they assumed. The Egyptian pantheon comprised deities who played major roles in the world. The building would also house some of the minor deities and some demons, foreign deities, and mortals (mainly dead kings).

The religious practices and rituals mainly revolved around the ruler of the country or its Pharaoh. The chosen ones, the pharaohs, were believed to have the power of the gods running through their veins, and their blood was sacred. They were chosen to maintain order in the mortal realm and could also help to bridge the boundary between humans and deities - temples would be built, rituals performed, and the deities would be revered. These Pharaohs were believed to be of the gods themselves, descending from the deities, thus able to commune with them the best. People could pray or use magic to interact directly with the gods. Over time, the power of the Pharaohs declined. This meant that personal spiritual practices held more meaning, substance, and power.

Cosmology

The ancient Egyptian universe was mainly built on the 7 principles of Maat. These principles hold numerous meanings and cannot be translated into English. They can be roughly translated to represent order, truth, justice, and virtue. Maat was everlasting and fixed. It could never be changed because the world would cease to exist without it. As anyone would expect, numerous threats - especially ones related to chaos and a lack of order- faced society. This meant that their society had to come together and make the effort needed to maintain Maat. It was believed to be replenished by recurrent events, including the annual flooding of the Nile river. It was thought that this event mirrored the start of creation.

Interestingly, ancient Egyptians believed that the Earth was flat. Geb represented the land, and his sister Nut represented the sky - in the middle was Shu, the air. Below Geb was a parallel universe that comprised the underworld and the undersky. Nu, the chaos that came before all creation, existed beyond the skies. Duat referred to a mysterious place that was linked to death and rebirth. This was the area that Ra journeyed through every day.

The Seven Maat Principles

The goddess Maat exhibited the principles of Maat - harmony, balance, justice, truth, reciprocity, order, and propriety. It was believed that all members of society, especially the Pharaohs and their relatives, should embody or follow those principles. By allowing Maat to govern every aspect of life, including how people deal with others and how they act and behave, harmony and peace could be achieved. People who neglected these principles were considered outlaws, and the rulers who Maat did not guide were believed to be unfit for their role.

The truth refers to a person's ability to differentiate between what is real and what isn't. People who lived their truth behaved in a way that favored the greater good. The truth refers to the belief that all living beings are sacred and deserving of respect. Justice was associated with not only social equity but equity between nature and all living beings. Rulers were expected to be just and had to ensure that the basic needs of everyone were met.

Harmony refers to the state in which all living beings interact and align beautifully with one another. It was related to authenticity and freedom of expression. The state of balance refers to when a person's internal and external environments align. Order was associated with organization and clarity.

Reciprocity is quite similar to the concept of karma. Your actions, whether good or bad, will be met with the appropriate reward or consequence. In other words, "What goes around comes around." Finally, propriety was the expectation that a person would do whatever was right. It meant a person should not hurt a living being, including themselves.

The Afterlife

Ancient Egyptians believed that the ka, or a person's life-force energy, continued to live on even after an individual's death. Since they were very concerned with an individual's fate following their death, they built tombs and provided food offerings to the deceased. It was also believed that the ba, or a person's spiritual traits, also lived on. This is why they conducted funeral rites to ensure the release of the ba so it could rejoin the ka. They were both expected to live on as akh. They practiced mummification techniques to preserve the deceased's body because they thought the ba returned to the body each night.

A ritual was conducted to determine where the soul of the deceased would go. Those who had passed would arrive in Maat's great hall, and it is there where their heart would be weighed. They would face Ren and the forty-two judges and have all their sins told to them. Once they had listened to all of their sins, their heart would be weighed. The heart was weighed against a feather to determine if it was heavy with sin or pure and light. If balanced with the feather, the individual was allowed to enter Aaru or heaven. If it was heavier, their soul was thought to have been destroyed forever.

Like in numerous ancient and modern-day cultures, traditions, and religions, the sun was a highly significant entity in ancient Egyptian culture. This symbol of renewal and light never failed to illuminate the vast lands of Egypt. It makes sense that the ancient Egyptians believed it to be the best-fitting symbol for the creator of the entire world. Where there is no sun, there is no life.

Chapter 3: Major Female Deities

One of the many fascinating aspects of Ancient Egyptian culture was their deities. Religion was a big part of ancient Egypt, and it was incorporated into various areas of their lives. Consequently, their deities were held in very high regard, and they constantly appeased them by presenting them with offerings and performing certain rituals. The ancient Egyptians were polytheistic since they worshiped more than one deity. There were various gods and goddesses in their culture. Female deities were highly respected as women played a vital role in society and were treated equally to their male counterparts. This chapter will focus on major female deities in ancient Egypt.

Isis, Goddess of Magic and Healing

Isis, goddess of magic and healing.
Jeff Dahl, CC BY-SA 4.0 <https://creativecommons.org/licenses/by-sa/4.0>, via Wikimedia Commons: https://commons.wikimedia.org/wiki/File:Isis.svg

Hieroglyphic Name

Isis was called ꜣst in ancient Egypt. The name translates to "female of the throne," which refers to her being the "queen of the throne." This is clear from her illustrations which featured a throne emblem on her head. Her name also indicated her prominent role as a royal deity. Since the ancient Egyptians omitted vowels, it is hard to know exactly how her name was pronounced. However, after further research, it is believed that her name was pronounced as ooh-saht.

Worshiping Isis

Isis wasn't only worshiped in ancient Egypt. After Alexander the Great conquered the country, more people became aware of the goddess, and the number of her worshippers grew. The ancient Greeks associated Isis with their goddess of agriculture, Demeter, while the ancient Romans linked her to their goddess of love, Venus. There were people in Asia, Britain, Israel, Turkey, Afghanistan, and Syria who also worshiped the goddess. Various temples throughout the Mediterranean were built in her honor to appease her. To this day, there are still pagans who revere Isis.

Symbols

- Throne
- Cow's horns and solar disk
- The knot of Isis (an ancient Egyptian symbol that means life)
- Sistrum rattle (a musical instrument that wards off evil spirits)
- Wings

Correspondences

- Fertility
- Motherhood
- Magic
- Rebirth
- Healing
- Death
- Water
- The color green

Myth

Isis was married to Osiris, the god of the underworld. Osiris and Isis wanted to help mankind become more civilized. Isis worked with her husband to better educate Egyptian women so they could live and thrive. Seth, who was Isis and Osiris's brother and the god of disorder, murdered Osiris so that he himself could become king. Isis didn't know what had happened to her husband, and she looked for him everywhere. When she found him and brought his body back to Egypt, Seth dismembered him and scattered the pieces worldwide. Loyal and devoted, Isis didn't give up and transformed into a bird to look for her husband's parts. With the help of her sister Nephthys, they found Osiris's parts and put them back together. Using her magic, Isis made her husband whole again, but he was a mummy, neither living nor dead. Other gods were impressed by Isis's devotion and determination to find her husband.

Connecting with Isis

If you want to connect with Isis, you should build an altar for her in your home. It is really simple. Just choose an undisturbed area and hang a picture or place a statue of her and light a candle. Since she is associated with the color green, you can also plant a small garden and dedicate it to her.

Offerings

- Sunflowers
- Daisies
- Lotus
- Red roses
- White roses
- Milk
- Wine
- Cinnamon oil
- Jasmine oil
- Sandalwood oil
- Honey
- Peanuts

- Grapes
- Chocolate
- Coconuts
- Moonstone
- Diamond
- Gold
- Pearl
- Anything green, gold, blue, red, and white

Signs Isis Is Calling You

Isis may appear in your dreams, or you may hear or see her name on TV or online. You may have the urge to work with the sun and moon. Kites and cows will start showing up in your daily life. You may receive one of her symbols as a gift. You will see them in dreams or in reality.

The Experience of Connecting with Isis

Many women have found ways to connect with Isis. The goddess usually calls to all women, specifically mothers and widows. When they answer her call, she can help them follow their intuition, learn to trust, and heal, and she can also provide guidance.

Maat, the Goddess of Justice and Truth

Maat, goddess of justice and truth.
No machine-readable author provided. Jeff Dahl assumed (based on copyright claims)., CC BY-SA 4.0 <https://creativecommons.org/licenses/by-sa/4.0>, via Wikimedia Commons: https://commons.wikimedia.org/wiki/File:Maat.svg

Hieroglyphic Name

Maat was spelled m3't in ancient Egyptian. The name means "That which is straight," which refers to justice, harmony, and order.

Worshiping Maat

Maat was worshiped all over ancient Egypt. However, we can say that she was and still is worshiped worldwide. Maat was considered a concept rather than a real deity. She didn't represent justice. She is justice, truth, and harmony. Since many people have lived by these concepts to this day, it is easy to assume that we all follow Maat's principles.

Symbols

- Ostrich feather
- Ankh (key of life)
- Scepter
- Wings
- Scales
- Turquoise

Correspondences

- Cosmic order
- Harmony
- Truth
- Justice

Myth

Maat played a huge role in ancient Egyptian mythology. She was the daughter of Ra, the creator deity and the god of the sun. Maat was born at the same moment Ra created the world. Her essence was infused with the universe, and all creation has lived according to her principles ever since. She brought comic order to an empty and chaotic world. The concept of Maat was represented in various Egyptian myths. Maat played a role in the story of Isis. She and her twin sister Nephthys represented life and death, respectively. Nephthys wasn't evil, but both sisters balanced each other just like lightness and darkness. In other words, they both represented comic balance, Maat.

Connecting with Maat

Guided meditation is one of the best ways to connect you with Maat. It is recommended that you hold a white feather in your hand while meditating.

- Find a quiet spot and sit in a comfortable position.
- Close your eyes and visualize yourself entering a holy chamber in an ancient Egyptian temple.
- Maat welcomes you with scales in her hands.
- You place your heart on her scale.
- Maat will weigh your heart against the feather of truth.
- If your heart is heavier than a feather, Maat will tell you what negative emotion is consuming your heart, like anger, envy, resentment, ... etc.
- If you are willing to release these emotions, she will place her hand over your heart, and a divine white light will shine from it through your heart.
- Your heart will be lighter than a feather.
- She will place your heart in your chest.
- She will ask you to replace all the negative emotions you released with positive ones like love, compassion, and forgiveness.

Offerings

- Chicken
- Fish
- Cold water
- Eggplant
- Olive oil
- Tea with milk
- Vinegar
- Hummus
- Almonds
- Scales

- Gold jewelry
- Clear quartz
- White marble
- Wine
- Fragrant incense

Signs Maat Is Calling You

Maat may appear in your dreams, or you may hear or come across her name in various places, like on TV or in a book. White feathers may begin showing up in your life.

The Experience of Connecting with Maat

People usually call on Maat when there is chaos and instability in their lives. Her followers usually experience harmony afterward as she brings unity and balance back into their lives.

Bastet, Goddess of Cats and Protection

Bastet, goddess of cats and protection.
Gunawan Kartapranata, CC BY-SA 3.0 <https://creativecommons.org/licenses/by-sa/3.0>, via Wikimedia Commons: https://commons.wikimedia.org/wiki/File:Bastet.svg

Hieroglyphic Name

Bastet was spelled b'stt in ancient Egyptian. Historians believe she used to be called Bast, "soul of Auset." Auset was another name for Bastet's mother, Isis. Egyptian priests later changed her name to Bastet, which means "She of the ointment jar." For this reason, her name is written with the Hieroglyphic symbol for an ointment jar.

Worshiping Bastet

Bastet was worshiped all over Egypt, specifically in Lower Egypt. The Greeks linked her to the goddess Artemis, and she became the goddess of the moon. There are still people who worship Bastet, and her cults are alive and active in several countries. Nowadays, Bastet followers worship her as the goddess of fertility.

Symbols

- Cats
- Lioness
- Solar disk
- Sistrum (ancient Egyptian musical instrument)
- Ointment Jar

Correspondences

- Fertility
- Home
- Childbirth
- Women's secrets
- Domesticity

Myth

Prince Setna, King Rameses' son, stole The Book of Thoth, a magic book written by Thoth, the god of knowledge and writing. One day, Setna saw a very beautiful woman and offered her money to sleep with her. The woman, called Tabubu, was the daughter of a Bastet priest. She agreed to have an affair with the prince, but he had to be discreet because she was a lady of ranking. When arriving to meet the prince, Tabubu had one condition before they began their affair. He had to sign over to her everything he owned. Setna, consumed by lust, agreed and made the deal right away.

Tabubu changed into a robe that showcased all her beautiful physical features to entice Setna. She made another condition that he had to sign over his children's possessions, and he obliged. She made one last request that Setna should kill his children. He agreed and gave the order right away. As Setna approached Tabubu and touched her, she screamed very loudly and disappeared.

Tabubu wasn't the daughter of a priest but a manifestation of the goddess Bastet. She was punishing Setna for angering the gods and stealing the Book of Thoth. However, Bastet wasn't so cruel. There is a version of this story where Setna repented after he lost everything and returned The Book of Thoth. When he arrived home, his children were alive and well.

Connecting with Bastet

Building an altar under the goddess's name will help you connect with her. Decorate the altar with rattles, baskets, brightly colored crystals, and pictures of lions and cats. Offering a prayer through singing and dancing will also help you connect with the deity. For pregnant women or those who hope to get pregnant and require Bastet protection, you can make an offering.

Offerings

- Chocolate
- Honey
- Perfumed ointment
- Milk
- Statues of cats
- Raw meat
- Catnip herbs
- Wine

Signs Bastet Is Calling You

The cat goddess will call on you using her favorite pet. Cats may follow you, and you may see them wherever you go. You may feel connected to a stray cat and may even adopt it. A friend may give you a gift with a cat image on it, or you randomly open a book and you land on a cat picture. Bastet may also appear in your dreams. You may also hear meowing when there are no cats around or simply feel the goddess's presence.

The Experience of Connecting with Bastet

Bastet followers believe that the goddess is always watching over their cats. When they connect with her, they feel that their cats are being protected.

Sekhmet, Goddess of War

Sekhmet, goddess of war.

Hieroglyphic Name

Sekhmet is pronounced ˈsɛkˌmɛt. It comes from the word "Sekhem," which means "powerful." Sekhmet means "She who is powerful."

Worshiping Sekhmet

Sekhmet was worshiped in Egypt in the Delta, Luxor, Letopolis, and Memphis. She is still highly revered and worshiped to this day, as many people consider her one of the most prominent pagan deities.

Symbols

- Red linen
- Lioness
- Sun disk
- Ankh
- Blood
- Fire
- Desert
- Red, orange, and yellow crystals
- The colors gold, red, and orange

Correspondences

- Healers
- Healing
- Medicine
- Chaos
- War
- Plague
- Hot desert

Myth

Sekhmet was Ra's daughter, who he created from fire. He became angry with mankind because they weren't following Maat's principles. So, he sent his daughter Sekhmet to punish them. To Ra's surprise, Sekhmet was hungry for blood and caused carnage. Egypt was covered in blood. When Ra saw the state of his people, he repented for his actions. He ordered Sekhmet to stop immediately. However, the goddess wouldn't listen to him as she was consumed with bloodlust. Ra decided to take action to save his people. He poured thousands of bear jugs and permanganate juice into Sekhmet's path. She thought it was blood and consumed all of it. She was so drunk that she passed out for three days.

There are two versions of this story's ending. One said that when she woke up, she was calm, and her bloodthirst was gone. Another said that when she opened her eyes, she saw Ptah, the god of creation. She fell in love with him right away. As she was the goddess of war and chaos and he was the god of creation, their union brought back Maat (balance). She gave birth to a son, Nefertum, who became the god of healing. When Matt was established, humanity was saved.

Connecting with Sekhmet

You can connect with Sekhmet through meditation. Light a candle, use some incense, sit in a comfortable position in a quiet spot, and close your eyes.

- Take a few deep breaths and relax your body.
- Set your intention, in your head or out loud, to connect with Sekhmet.
- Imagine you are in a desert on a very hot summer day.

- You see the pyramids far away, and you walk toward them.
- It isn't an easy journey since the sun is blazing hot.
- You arrive and walk into the middle pyramid.
- It is quiet inside, with beautiful paintings and symbols.
- You find a door, and it slides open for you.
- A voice comes from the inside saying, "enter."
- There is a beautiful woman sitting on a throne who asks you who you are.
- You tell her your name and that you are here to connect with Sekhmet.
- She nods and informs you that she is Sekhmet.
- There is silence in the room.
- Moments later, the goddess stands up and begins talking to you.
- Listen to what she is saying, ask questions, and connect with her.
- When you have finished your conversation, she will leave the room.
- Take a few deep breaths, and then open your eyes.

You can also connect with her by creating an altar indoors or outdoors and decorating it with her symbols.

Offerings
- Music
- Food
- Drinks
- Burning incense

Signs Sekhmet Is Calling You

Sekhmet may call on you by appearing to you in your dreams. You may also see her symbols in your dreams or reality. If you are focused, you might feel her guidance.

The Experience of Connecting with Sekhmet

People usually call on Sekhmet when they need courage and strength to speak up or stand up for themselves. When they connect with her, they feel strong, empowered, and able to speak their truth.

Serqet, Goddess of the Dead and Healing Stings

Serqet, goddess of the dead and healing stings.
Jeff Dahl, CC BY-SA 4.0 <https://creativecommons.org/licenses/by-sa/4.0>, via Wikimedia Commons: https://commons.wikimedia.org/wiki/File:Serket.svg

Hieroglyphic Name

Serqet is pronounced ˈsɜːrˌkɛt. Her name means "She who causes the throat to breathe." This refers to her ability to cure snakes and scorpion stings.

Worshiping Serqet

Serqet was mainly worshiped in Lower Egypt.

Symbols

- The Ankh
- The Was Scepter (a Hieroglyphic symbol for power)
- Scorpions

Correspondences

- Magic
- Healing
- Protection

Myth

Serqet was one of the goddesses of the underworld. Ra would travel to the underworld every night, which wasn't a safe journey. The goddess would watch over him and make sure there weren't any dangers in his path. There was a serpent called Apep, who was an evil spirit that caused destruction. He was also one of Ra's arch-enemies. Serqet restrained Apep in the underworld and protected anyone journeying through the underworld from him. She also protected Isis when she gave birth to her son Horus. Isis was afraid that Seth would find them and her husband's fate would befall her son. Serqet watched over Isis when she was giving birth and kept Horus safe. In so many ways, Serqet is considered a protector.

Connecting with Serqet

You can connect with Serqet by building an altar in her name. You can decorate the altar with the key to life and images or statues of the goddess.

Offerings

- Bloodstone crystal
- Citrine
- Amethyst
- Garnet
- Cayenne pepper
- Angelica root
- Cannabis
- Cinnamon
- Anything in gold, purple, or red

Signs Serqet Is Calling You

Similar to the various goddesses we have already mentioned, Serqet may appear to you in your dreams, or you may feel her presence around you.

The Experience of Connecting with Serqet

People who are recovering from substance abuse call on Serqet for her detoxification and healing abilities. It is believed that Serqet gives them strength through these hard times. Usually, when we are at our weakest, we look for a higher power to help get us out of adversity. Serqet is a protector and a healer who can give you the support you need.

Neith Goddess of War and Creation

Neith, goddess of war and creation.
Jeff Dahl, CC BY-SA 4.0 <https://creativecommons.org/licenses/by-sa/4.0>, via Wikimedia Commons: https://commons.wikimedia.org/wiki/File:Neith.svg

Hieroglyphic Name

Neith's original name is believed to have been Nrt which means "She, the terrifying one," since she was one of the most powerful deities.

Worshiping Neith

Neith was worshiped all over Egypt, but her most loyal followers were in Lower Egypt.

Symbols

- Sword
- Shield
- Bow and arrow
- Weaving shuttle
- Red crown of Lower Egypt
- Ankh
- Scepter

- Spider
- Cows

Correspondences

- War
- Wisdom
- Creation
- Weaving
- Water and rivers
- The cosmos
- Mothers
- Hunting
- Childbirth
- Fate

Myth

When Isis's son Horus grew up, he was ready to take his place as the rightful king of Egypt. He argued with Ra and the assembly of gods that, as Osiris's son, he should be king rather than his uncle Seth. Naturally, Seth opposed it. When Ra heard both sides, he felt that Horus wasn't ready to be king. He was young and didn't have enough experience. However, the other gods were on Horus's side.

The gods couldn't make a decision, so they enlisted the help of the wisest deity, Neith. She decided that Horus was the rightful king and should take his place on the throne. However, she was still fair and compensated Seth with two wives.

Connecting with Neith

You can build an altar for Neith indoors or outdoors. Decorate it with images or statues of the goddesses. You can also add ankhs, a small bow and an arrow, and toy cows and spiders.

Offerings

- Cool water
- Bread
- Dates

- Onions

Signs Neith Is Calling You

You may either have a dream or a vision of Neith. You may also start seeing her symbols in your daily life. For instance, a spider may crawl into your backyard when you don't have spiders in your area, or you will see a cow a few times on your way to work. You may also see a red crown, sword, or shield or be given the key to life as a gift.

The Experience of Connecting with Neith

People who have connected with Neith have mentioned how motherly and protective she was.

There are so many things that we can learn from female Egyptian deities. Just keep your heart, eyes, and mind open as one may be calling out to you. If not, connect with them using the methods we have covered here.

Chapter 4: Major Male Deities

Now that you have learned about the major female deities in ancient Egypt, we will take a look at the male gods. Male deities are as prominent in Egyptian mythology as their female counterparts. Their lives are filled with fascinating stories that can help you not only learn about their characteristics but also know which deity you can call on when you need guidance.

Ra, the Creator and the God of the Sun

Ra, the creator and god of the sun.
Jeff Dahl, CC BY-SA 4.0 <https://creativecommons.org/licenses/by-sa/4.0>, via Wikimedia Commons: https://commons.wikimedia.org/wiki/File:Re-Horakhty.svg

Hieroglyphic Name

Ra was called r' in ancient Egypt, and it is pronounced ra:. The name means "sun." He also went by multiple other names; Atum, Khepri, Ra-Horakhty, Re, Pra, and Amun-Re. Ra also had another name that no one was allowed to learn since it was the secret to his divine power. When Isis tried to find out his secret name, he revealed some of his other names but not the ones she wanted to know. He said, "I am Khepera in the morning, Ra at noon-day, and Temu in the evening," which gave us an idea of some of the deity's other names.

Worshiping Ra

Ra was worshiped all over ancient Egypt. It is believed that his worship began in an Egyptian town called Iunu in Northern Cairo. When the Greeks conquered Egypt, they named the town Heliopolis, which means "city of the sun of god." Thousands of years later, the city of Heliopolis is still standing, and its name remains unchanged. Ra is still revered, and some people worship him and believe he has always been the supreme god since he created the world.

Symbols

- Solar disk
- Scepter
- Ankh
- The sun
- Scarab beetle
- Falcon
- Boat
- Eye of Ra
- Ram
- Lion
- Cobra

Correspondences

- The sun
- Creation
- Earth

- Heaven
- The underworld
- The sky
- Balance
- Destruction
- Justice
- Royalty
- Healing
- Vengeance
- Vitality
- Prosperity
- Protection
- Enlightenment

Myth

Before the world was created, there was only darkness. The only thing that existed was water which was called Nun. Ra created himself out of Nun. According to one version of this legend, he was able to bring himself to life by uttering his own name, and, in another version, he came into existence by an effort of will. Next came the twins: Tefnut and Shu. The world was still dark since there was no sunlight or moonlight, so Ra could not find his children. Consequently, Ra created an eye to help him look for his new children. The eye left to find the new gods, but it discovered an unpleasant surprise when it returned. Ra had created another eye in its absence.

The first eye was very angry and felt betrayed. Ra made the first eye stronger than the second to quell its rage. The stronger of the two transformed into the sun, and the weaker transformed into the moon. For this reason, the sun was referred to as "the eye of Ra." After that, Ra created celestial bodies, gods, and goddesses. There are various stories about how Ra created humanity. One story says that he wept after creating the gods and his tears became mankind. Another story says that he created the world by uttering everything by its secret name. While there is a story that says after the first eye discovered that Ra created a second one, it cried out of rage, and in another version, it cried out of loneliness, and its tears became humanity.

The one thing that all these stories share in common is that humanity was created out of loneliness, anger, and misery. In many ways, this story is a similar interpretation of mankind and the condition of the world, which has remained unchanged for centuries.

Connecting with Ra

As mentioned, building an altar is one of the most effective methods to help you connect with a deity. Simply choose a small space in your home, like a shelf or a table. Place images, statues, or crystals related to Ra or ancient Egypt. You can also add candles or incense. Since Ra is the god of the sun, the best times to connect with him are at sunrise, sunset, and high noon. So cast your spells, and practice yoga or meditation at these times.

Offerings

- Water
- Frankincense
- Candlelight
- Beer
- Bread
- Fruit
- Poultry
- Gold
- Linen

Signs Ra Is Calling You

As mentioned in the previous chapters, gods usually call on us in our dreams either by appearing themselves or sending us their symbols. You may see the sun, a falcon, or a scarab beetle in your dreams. You may also hear the name Ra or keep finding things related to the sun in dreams or reality. For instance, a friend may give you a sun necklace, or you may keep finding posts about the Sun or Ra online.

The Experience of Connecting with Ra

Ra's followers often call on him when they need balance in their lives since he is the god of creation and destruction. Ra also protects people who seek justice, like judges, juries, lawyers, police officers, etc.

Osiris, the God of Life and Death

Osiris, god of life and death.

Jeff Dahl, CC BY-SA 4.0 <https://creativecommons.org/licenses/by-sa/4.0>, via Wikimedia Commons: https://commons.wikimedia.org/wiki/File:Standing_Osiris_edit1.svg

Hieroglyphic Name

Osiris used to be called wsjr in hieroglyphic, which was pronounced as jsjrj because hieroglyphs didn't have any vowels. Egyptologists later changed the vocalization of the name to Usir, which is pronounced as "oos-ee-r." Osiris is the Greek version of the name. The name translates to "powerful" or "mighty," which makes it an appropriate name for one of the most prominent gods in ancient Egypt.

Worshiping Osiris

Many people worshiped Osiris throughout ancient Egypt, and his main followers were from Abydos, an ancient city in Upper Egypt. He was the god of death, and the ancient Egyptians believed in life after death, so Osiris was regarded as a deity who could grant life after death. As a result, he was revered in other places worldwide, like Rome and Greece. The Greeks associated him with their own god of the underworld, Hades.

Symbols

- Mummy gauze
- Crook and flail (symbols of royalty)

- Green skin
- Atef crown (feathered white crown)
- Ostrich feathers
- Djed (represents power and stability)

Correspondences

- The underworld
- Death
- Strength
- Fertility
- Agriculture
- Resurrection
- Flood
- The cycle of the Nile

Myth

We mentioned Osiris in the previous chapter. He was Isis's husband, who his brother Seth killed and dismembered. Osiris became the god of the underworld when Isis brought him back. He was a mummy, neither dead nor alive. However, before he became the god of the underworld, he was the god of agriculture. Legend has it that the ancient Egyptians used to be cannibals until Osiris introduced agriculture to them. That said, historians argue that this myth is lacking, and there is no real evidence to support it. Still, Osiris is credited for bringing agriculture, order, and civilization to a chaotic and uncivilized world.

Looking at illustrations of Osiris, you will see that he was depicted with a kind smile. This shows that he was a good and approachable god. The people loved and respected him and didn't fear him like other gods. He only wanted to help mankind. When he became the god of the underworld, he made sure that justice and order prevailed.

Connecting with Osiris

Building an altar for Osiris will help you connect with him. Decorate the altar with images or statues of the god or by using any of his symbols like the crook and flail or the Atef crown. You can also try visualization and meditation while holding an ostrich feather if you can find one.

Offerings

- Bread
- Vegetables (except lettuce)
- Beer
- Wine
- Dark chocolate
- Brandy
- Scotch
- Apples
- Seeds
- Real plants
- Aquamarine
- Frankincense
- Colors: green, purple, brown, and black

Signs Osiris Is Calling You

Osiris will appear in your dreams if he wants to connect with you. He may not come himself, though. You may hear his name in your dreams or see his symbols.

The Experience of Connecting with Osiris

People who connected with Osiris felt that he was extremely focused and a little stern. However, he was good-natured, and he had a sense of humor.

Horus, the God of the Sky

Horus, god of the sky.

Hieroglyphic Name

Horus's name used to be spelled as ḥr.w, which meant falcon. It later came to be pronounced as ˈħaːɾuw then as ˈħaːɾəʔ. The name went through different pronunciations over the years, and it was the ancient Greeks who called him Hōros, which is pronounced hôːros. The name is believed to have had other meanings in Latin, like "One who is above, over" or "the distant one," which obviously refers to his role as the god of the sky.

Worshiping Horus

Horus was worshiped all over Egypt, and there was a temple for him in Upper Egypt. Back in the day, ancient Egypt was split in two, and Horus was only worshiped in Southern Egypt. When the North and South were reunited, he was the Pharaoh of united Egypt. There are still, to this day, people who worship ancient Egyptian deities, including Horus. He was also worshiped in Greece. Several pagans still honor him and include him in their practices.

Symbols

- Falcon's head
- Eye of Horus
- Hawk
- Peacock

Correspondences

- The Sky
- War
- The sun
- The moon
- Protection

Myth

We mentioned in the last chapter how Horus became a king. However, there is more than one version of this story. Horus wasn't only concerned about the throne. He also wanted to avenge his father. He and Seth fought on more than one occasion. During one of these fights, Seth blinded Horus in his left eye. Thoth, the god of the moon and writing, healed him. His new eye was named wedjat, which became "The eye of Horus" and a symbol of protection. He became more adamant than ever about killing Seth, which he eventually did, and he finally avenged his father. After Seth's death, Horus became king.

Another story states that when the gods couldn't decide between Horus and Seth, instead of seeking Neith's help, Set and Horus were to undertake certain contests to determine which one of them was fit to be the king. In one of the contests, they turned into hippopotamuses and were supposed to go underwater to see who could stay there the longest. When underwater, Isis could have killed Seth, but she didn't. Horus was understandably angry with his mother, and he left to stay in the desert. Seth found him, and this time he took out both of his eyes. However, Hathor, the goddess of fertility, healed him and made him whole again.

Eventually, the gods decided that Horus should be king since he won almost all the contests and proved himself worthy of the throne. Horus had shown courage, skill, honor, and determination in all versions.

Connecting with Horus

You can paint or draw the eye of Horus to connect with him and gain his protection. You can also create an altar and add statues and images of the deity and his eye. Wearing the Eye of Horus as an amulet may also help. Since he is the god of the sky, spend some time outdoors looking at the sky and thinking of Horus.

Offerings

- Bread
- Triangular cakes
- Iron
- Fresh red meat
- Incense
- Bread
- Cool water
- Candles
- Beer

Signs Horus Is Calling You

If Horus is calling you, he will appear in your dream, or you will see a hawk or a falcon in your dreams or real life. A friend may also give you an eye of Horus amulet as a gift.

The Experience of Connecting with Horus

When connecting with Horus, it is vital that you keep in mind that he is both a god and a king. So, treat him according to his rank and address him with respect. People who connect with him also feel he has become their guide and is always there with them as they constantly see falcons and Hawks. He also seems to be caring and protective.

Set the God of the Desert and Chaos

Set, god of the desert and chaos.
Jeff Dahl (talk · contribs), CC BY-SA 4.0 <https://creativecommons.org/licenses/by-sa/4.0>, via Wikimedia Commons: https://commons.wikimedia.org/wiki/File:Set.svg

Hieroglyphic Name

Set is the god Seth whom we have mentioned a few times in the book. The Greeks were the ones who gave him the name Seth. In Hieroglyphics, it was spelled as sth and swth and pronounced 'suw tix[j]. The meaning of the name remains a mystery.

Worshiping Set

Set was mainly worshiped in Upper Egypt. People found him admirable since he was strong and cunning. However, after he killed his brother, many of his followers began to regard him in a negative light. Even the Greeks associated him with an evil force. Only in some areas of Egypt was he regarded as a chief deity. Set represents chaos and power, traits many people gravitate toward, which is why a few pagans still worship him.

Symbols

- Set animal
- Was Scepter

Correspondences

- Disorder
- Infertility
- Desert
- Storms
- Violence

Myth

We have mentioned Set a few times, and he appeared as the villain in all of them. He killed his brother and tried to kill his nephew. So, what drove Set to these actions? Set was always jealous of Osiris but what prompted him to murder his brother wasn't just his jealousy. His wife, Nephthys, transformed into Isis and slept with Osiris. They had a son Annubis, the god of the dead. When Set found out about this betrayal, he killed his brother. However, Set's anger was misplaced since Osiris thought she was his wife.

In one of the versions of the story where Horus became king, and Set was compensated by marrying two women, who were Ra's daughters, Ra offered Set a job. He would protect Ra's boat from the evil serpent Apep.

Connecting with Set

You can connect with Set by creating an altar or meditating. Some people connect with him by honoring him on his birthday. Get a red candle, carve his hieroglyphic name, and light it. Add to the altar any orange, yellow, or red items. Honoring Set on his birthday can help you develop a personal relationship with him.

Offerings

- Lettuce
- Red stones
- Cinnamon
- Handmade art
- Sandalwood
- Spicy food

Signs Set Is Calling You

You may see Set in your dreams if you sleep facing north. Someone may mention Set's name in your dream, or you may hear it on TV or see it online.

The Experience of Connecting with Set

People who connected with Set often compared him to the Norse god of chaos and mischief, Loki. For this reason, they always approach this prankster deity with caution. His followers don't find him evil. In fact, they find him a great god to work with.

Thoth the God of the Moon and Writing

Thoth, god of the moon and writing.
Jeff Dahl, CC BY-SA 4.0 <https://creativecommons.org/licenses/by-sa/4.0>, via Wikimedia Commons: https://commons.wikimedia.org/wiki/File:Thoth.svg

Hieroglyphic Name

Thoth's original name was Djehuty which is pronounced as *Je-hu-ti*. His name translates to "He who is like the Ibis," which is a type of bird that the god is depicted as. It is a common bird in Ancient Egypt and has come to be associated with wisdom. His name was written in various ways, like Jehuti, Tetu, Tahuti, and Tahuti. Thoth was often referred to as "Lord of divine words" and "Lord of Maat." It was the Greeks who referred to him as Thoth, which is the name commonly used.

Worshiping Thoth

Thoth was mainly worshiped in Upper Egypt, as his cult originated in a town called Khmunu. The Greeks referred to this town as Hermopolis, which is now called Al-Ashmūnayn. They associated Thoth with their god Hermes since both deities were considered messengers of the gods. The Greeks revered and highly admired him and considered him the source of all knowledge. There are still people around the world, including in America, who worship Thoth.

Symbols

- Ibis
- Scales
- Moon disk
- Baboon
- Papyrus scroll
- Writing palette
- Stylus
- Red pen

Correspondences

- Divine balance
- The moon
- Writing
- Learning
- Reckoning
- Wisdom

- Magic
- Healing
- Language

Myth

There is more than one story about Thoth's birth. One says that, like Ra, he also created himself. In another story, he was born from Ra's lips. In a different one, he was born from Set's forehead. We have mentioned that Thoth healed Horus's eye. However, Thoth was fair and didn't side with either of the conflicting deities. He also healed Set on multiple occasions. He wanted the contests between the gods to remain fair and refused to give one an advantage over another.

One of Ra's eyes, who was also his daughter, disagreed with him and decided to leave. Ra was unable to see when his eye disappeared and decided to send someone after her to bring her back. However, bringing her back wasn't going to be an easy task since she was so strong, and no one would be able to force her. This mission didn't only require someone who was physically strong but also smart and cunning.

In ancient Egyptian mythology, the goddess is often referred to as the distant goddess, and it was Thoth that Ra chose to bring her back. He disguised himself as a monkey and went after the goddess. In one version of the story, Thoth asked her to go back home about 1,077 times. He was cunning and persistent and didn't give up until he succeeded in his mission and brought her home. Ra was delighted by Thoth's success and awarded him the goddess Nehemtawy to be his consort.

Connecting with Thoth

To connect with Toth, research and learn as much as possible about him. Thoth admires learning, curiosity, and knowledge. You can also pray to him by setting up an altar and decorating it with ibis origami or statues.

Offerings

- Cool water
- Honey
- Orange juice

- Lemons
- Blackberries
- Apricots
- Chicken
- Tuna
- Salmon
- Lamb's ribs
- Onion
- Garlic
- Walnuts
- Quills
- Ibis feather
- Papyrus
- Pen
- Poetry

Signs Thoth Is Calling You

You may see the name Thoth everywhere. People may be posting stuff about him online, seeing his name in books, or hearing people talk about him. He or his symbols may also appear to you in your dreams. You may also feel connected to him or curious about him. Fulfill this curiosity and learn more about him because he loves curiosity.

The Experience of Connecting with Thoth

Some people call on Thoth when they experience writer's block or have an exam. According to them, the god is always happy to help, and since you will learn so much from him, they advise you to show gratitude and present offerings.

The gods of ancient Egypt have always been known for their wisdom. You can learn and grow once you begin working with them. Learn about the deities and choose the one who can help and guide you on your journey.

Chapter 5: Egyptian Symbols and Their Significance

Religion was a big part of ancient Egypt. Their gods played a huge role throughout their lives and even after death by helping them transition into the afterlife. The gods were always there to take care of mankind. For this reason, the physical and spiritual worlds were often intertwined with each other. This was clear from the presence of various symbols in their illustrations, objects, architecture, and amulets, especially the objects used by clergymen and the nobility. These symbols were very beneficial and practical for several reasons.

Like many other societies at the time, the ancient Egyptians were illiterate. Symbols provided a method for people from all walks of life to read hymns and poetry and communicate with one another. Symbols also had a magical significance and were used in various spells and rituals. This chapter will cover the most prominent Egyptian symbols and their significance.

The Ankh

Ankh symbol.
https://commons.wikimedia.org/wiki/File:Ankh-Symbol.svg

The Ankh is a very popular symbol. In fact, many people today wear it as jewelry or tattoo it over their bodies without realizing its meaning or knowing its origins. The Ankh looks like a cross with a looped top. It resembles a key, and it can grant its holder the secrets of existence. The Ankh is often referred to as "the key to life," and it symbolizes eternal life. The ring on the top of the Ankh represents the joining of man and woman, the heavens and the mortal world, and the journey between the two worlds.

This symbol was very powerful, which is why the Pharaohs and the gods were often depicted holding it. It is also associated with the Knot of Isis and her cult. When Isis grew more popular, more people became aware of the Ankh. The origin of the Ankh remains a mystery.

The Ankh in the Past

According to various ancient artworks and illustrations, the gods in the afterlife who judged the spirits of the dead usually had an Ankh in their hand. They would bring it to the deceased's nostrils so they could breathe in immortality. It was also used during purification ceremonies for the Pharaohs. Water by chains of Ankhs would be presented to him and poured over his head. This served as a reminder that the Pharaoh ruled under the gods and that they would return to him when he died.

The Ankh Today

Nowadays, people use the Ankh to bring prosperity, strength, and balance into their lives. Some Kemetic pagans use the Ankh as a symbol of their faith, and there are other worshippers from multiple faiths who see the Ankh as a symbol of life and wisdom. Isis followers use the ankh during their rituals as well.

The Djed Pillar

The Djed pillar is basically a column with a base that is broad, and it narrows as it rises. The top is easily recognized by its four parallel lines. The ancient Egyptians believed that these four lines represented the four corners of the planet. The number four was also heavily featured in ancient Egyptian mythology. They believed that it represented wholeness and completeness. The Djed pillar is often called "the Backbone of Osiris." It is associated with Osiris and symbolizes stability, strength, resurrection, and eternity. You can find this symbol in ancient Egyptian temples, amulets, and the book of the dead.

It is a symbol that is often connected to Isis and Osiris. It represented rebirth and resurrection, which was what Osiris experienced after Set murdered him. It acted as a fertility pole and was also linked to Osiris, who was the god of agriculture before becoming the god of the underworld. Osiris would flood the river Nile to fertilize the land.

The Djed Pillar in the Past

The ancient Egyptians used the Djed during their festivals. It acted as a fertility pole representing the balance between life and the afterlife. The Djed would be raised into the air to represent the rising crops, life rising from what once seemed dead, and the rising of a person's spirit from this realm to the next.

This symbol was also included on the bottom of coffins because it was associated with resurrection. The ancient Egyptians believed that it helped the deceased's soul stand and take its first steps toward the afterlife.

The Djed Pillar Today

You can include the Djedt in spells that will help bring balance and stability into your life.

The Eye of Horus/Wadjet

After Horus lost his left eye fighting with Set, Thoth restored it, and it was given the name Wadjet, and it protected Horus. For this reason, Wadjet became a symbol of healing and protection. It also represented good fortune, sacrifice, health, and royal power. The eye of Horus is one of ancient Egypt's most popular symbols.

The Eye of Horus in the Past

Wadjet was associated with magical abilities. The ancient Egyptians believed it was a powerful symbol with healing powers. For this reason, physicians at the time used it in their practices to measure the medicine ingredients. They also believed that it had immense mathematical knowledge.

The Eye of Horus Today

Nowadays, Wadject still represents similar themes as people associate it with protection, revelation, and wisdom. It is often compared to the eye of providence on the one-dollar bill. Some people associate it with control and manipulation since it resembles the symbol of the questionable group, the Illuminati. However, it is still regarded by many as a force for good. People use it to protect themselves against evil. They hang it in their homes as protection from physical and spiritual dangers. They also use it in various spells to attract positive energy and repel negative energy.

The Eye of Ra/The Udjat Eye

The eye of Ra is often linked to the Wadjet, as both were considered protective goddesses in ancient Egyptian mythology. The Udjat, as it was referred to, is often featured in various myths as the Distant Goddess we mentioned in the last chapter. There are different versions of this myth, but they all share one common theme, and that is the goddess ran away, and someone went after her to bring her back or trick her into coming back. The eye of Ra referred to either the

Distant Goddess herself or those who were sent to bring her back.

The symbol also acted as Ra's, the creator's watchful eye over mankind – representing power, authority, peace, and rebirth.

The Eye of Ra in the Past

Just like its counterpart, the Udjat was used to repel negative energies and bring harmony. The ancient Egyptians also used it to protect themselves and their homes. They would paint it over their homes to bring good health, repel evil spirits, and break harmful spells. Fishermen also painted it on their boats before they went fishing to protect themselves and their boats from evil spirits. The Eye of Ra was often used to protect the dead when they traveled to the next world.

The Eye of Ra Today

The eye of Ra is as popular today as it was thousands of years ago. It is used in Reiki to symbolize knowledge and enlightenment. People associate it with the Third Eye, which connects us to our truest selves. You can also wear it to protect yourself from the "evil eye" or people who wish you harm.

The Scarab

The scarab is a beetle that was extremely popular in ancient Egypt until the arrival of Christianity. You can find this symbol in artwork and illustrations. The scarab beetle is a type of dung beetle. The beetle would roll animal droppings into a ball and use them as breeding chambers for their eggs as it provided food for the young when the eggs hatched. When the ancient Egyptians saw this process, they associated the beetle with the gods since its lifecycle represented resurrection, creation of life, and transformation. The scarab was also associated with Khepri, the god of the morning sun, who had a face like a scarab beetle.

The Scarab in the Past

The letter of the scarab in hieroglyphics is linked to growth and transformation. For this reason, the ancient Egyptian used the scarab symbol to describe the ranks of officers in the government.

The Scarab Today

The ancient Egyptians associated the scarab with good luck. You can wear it as an amulet to bring good fortune into your life.

The Ka

The ka symbol means soul or spirit. Its hieroglyphic symbol is shoulders and arms bent and pointing upward at the elbow. It is associated with the new soul of an infant who is resurrected after death. Simply put, it was the essence of a person, and it had a huge impact on all areas of one's life. The gods were the ones to bestow ka among mankind since they were the ones that gave them life or the spirit. The ka of a royal was different from that of the people. The ka of royals was regarded as original or unique, while the soul of a regular person was of lesser value and belonged to the gods.

The Ka in the Past

The ancient Egyptians considered the ka a symbol of protection and acted as a guardian. It was responsible for making a person kind, compassionate, and honorable.

The Ka Today

People use the ka symbol because they believe it can put them on the right path in life.

The Ouroboros

The Ouroboros is one of the oldest Egyptian signs. It is probably as old as the creation of the universe. It was created when Ra willed himself into existence. When he first appeared, he took the form of a serpent which is why the Ouroboros symbol is a serpent eating its own tail. The symbol represents Ra's journeys and is associated with recreation and rebirth. The Ouroboros symbolizes the circle of life, time, death, fertility, and good luck.

The Ouroboros in the Past

Ouroboros was engraved in the tomb of Tutankhamen because it represented life after death. The symbol was a part of Norse and Greek mythology as well.

The Ouroboros Today

The Ouroboros is depicted as either a serpent or a dragon forming a circle and eating its own tail. It is usually associated with alchemy.

The Uraeus

A cobra represents the goddess of royalty, Wadjet, representing the authority of the divine, royalty, and sovereignty. According to ancient Egyptian mythology, the Uraeus symbolizes protection and has magical powers. In hieroglyphics, it was associated with a shrine.

The Uraeus in the Past

The Uraeus acted as a royal symbol to prove that the Pharaoh on the throne was the legitimate king. For that reason, kings are often depicted wearing the Uraeus symbol to prove their legitimacy. The goddess Wadjet offered protection to the Pharaoh wearing this symbol.

The Uraeus Today

People include the Uraeus in their rituals because it has magical powers. You can also wear it for protection.

The Was Scepter

The Was scepter is a staff with an animal head, often a canine, and a fork at the end. This symbol was heavily influenced by the Hekat scepter, which represented royal power. In ancient Egyptian legends, the color of the staff and the fork often changed depending on who was holding it. They believed that the sky was built on four Was scepters. The ancient Egyptians referred to it as the "sculptor of the earth." It represented completeness. Each god and goddess had their own scepters like Isis and Ra, and their concept changed according to the god who was holding it. For instance, when Isis held it, it became associated with fertility. When Ra held it, it represented rebirth, and when Horus held it, it was associated with the sky.

The Was Scepter in the Past

The ancient Egyptians used the Was scepter with the ankh and the Djed, as is clear from their illustrations. When combined together, these three symbols provide long life, strength, and success.

The Was Scepter Today

Some people use the Was scepter in magic rituals.

The Crook and Flail

The crook and flail represent the power of a king. They were symbols of the god Osiris and his rule over Egypt. These symbols are also related to Horus and his myth. When he defeated Set and took his place on the throne, he took Osiris's crook and flail to prove that he was the legitimate king.

The Crook and Flail in the Past

Before they became sacred symbols, the shepherds used the crook with their goats and harvested certain plants with the flail. Osiris became associated with these symbols because he was the god of agriculture. In addition to being symbols of a legitimate and powerful king, the crook and flail became reminders of the past and old traditions as well.

The Shen

The Shen is depicted as a circle made of a rope. The circle doesn't have a beginning or an end to illustrate wholeness and completeness. It is a symbol of infinity, eternity, divine protection, and an unbroken bond. The word "*shen*" means "encircle." This symbol is quite similar to the Greek omega symbol, which also represents infinity. In various illustrations, we can see gods and goddesses holding the Shen. Isis and Horus were often depicted holding one. As a result, ancient Egyptians held the symbol in high regard and considered it a symbol of perfection.

The Shen in the Past

Shen amulets were very popular in ancient Egypt. All Egyptians, from slaves to farmers to kings, wore one. They also engraved it on tombs and temples.

The Shen Today

If you are looking to feel whole or complete, you can wear this symbol of wholeness and completeness.

The Sesen

The Sesen symbol is a lotus flower often associated with ancient Egypt, representing life, creation, rebirth, and the sun. It was often compared to the sun because at night, the lotus flower closes and goes underwater, and, just like the sun, it emerges the next day. The life of the lotus represents very important themes like rebirth. It is also associated with Ra, who willed himself into existence by emerging from the water "nun." It is a symbol of rebirth, regeneration, enlightenment, and purity.

The Sensen in the Past

The lotus flower played a huge role in ancient Egyptian art as it was painted or engraved on amulets, shrines, and temples. It was also a symbol of Upper Egypt. This symbol was popular among the cult of Osiris, the god of the underworld. Its disappearance at night and emergence in the morning were linked to themes of death and resurrection.

The Lotus Today

The lotus flower is the main ingredient in many spells. The symbol itself can be used in various rituals that are associated with purity, cleanliness, or rebirth.

The Ben-Ben

Although you may be unfamiliar with the name ben-ben, you will most definitely recognize the symbol. The ben-ben are the pyramids of Egypt. Nothing is more associated with the country and its history than these famous monuments. The place where the pyramids stand is where creation began, as Ra stood there before he created mankind. The pyramids stand on the ground and rise toward the heavens. In one of the myths about creation, there was only darkness and chaos before the world came into existence. The pyramids or ben-ben were the first dry land created where Ra stood and began creating the world. For this reason, the pyramids were associated with creation.

The Ben-Ben in the Past

Ancient Egyptians wore the Ben-Ben symbol as an amulet, and they were crafted as statues and engraved on tombs and temples.

The Ben-Ben Today

The pyramids have always been mysterious and enchanting. There are people who believe that they have magical powers. As a result of their triangular shape, they can be used in healing rituals like healing the seven chakras.

The Feather of Maat

As mentioned in a previous chapter, Maat was either the goddess of justice or justice itself. She weighed the heart of the deceased against the feather of Maat to determine if they were good individuals who lived their lives in the service of others or led selfish lives. The feather of Matt is one of the most prominent symbols in ancient Egypt as it determines how people will spend their afterlife. Without the feather, it would be impossible to weigh the hearts, and thus the dead would have no place to go. Simply put, the feather of Maat was the foundation of the afterlife. Maat was associated with justice, order, harmony, balance, and truth.

The Feather of Maat in the Past

When the deceased reach the afterlife, they must stand in front of Osiris, where they will be judged by their heart being placed on a scale and weighed against a feather. If the heart's weight was lighter than the feather, it meant that they achieved good deeds when they were alive and deserved to spend eternity in the land of the field of the reeds, the equivalent to heaven or a good place. However, if the heart was heavier than the feather, they didn't lead a good or selfless life and would be devoured by the goddess Ammit, and they would cease to exist.

The Feather of Maat Today

The feather of Maat was a white ostrich feather. People who want to connect with Maat use an ostrich feather or any white feather when meditating to help them reach out to the goddess.

Ancient Egypt is filled with many secrets and mysteries. Their symbols are fascinating. Each one has a story behind it and can be used in various rituals and spells to this day. All these symbols can also be used to help you connect with your favorite deity. Since each god and goddess has their own symbols, you can learn about them and their myths and use them in meditation, decorate the deity's altar, tattoo them onto your body, or wear them as jewelry to keep the gods close to your heart.

Chapter 6: Egyptian Amulets and How to Make Them

Ancient Egyptian symbols held magical power. They were so powerful that they were also used as magical symbols in other belief systems and hermetic orders like the Rosicrucians.

These symbols don't simply have magical powers when written down. You can also create three-dimensional amulets of these symbols to aid you in your magical and religious practices.

If you're wondering how to create ancient Egyptian amulets, you're in the right place. In this chapter, you will explore the idea of ancient Egyptian amulets in greater detail, so you can understand why the Egyptians prized them. This chapter will also offer a few techniques to create your own amulets, which you can use in your spiritual and magical practice.

Understanding Ancient Egyptian Amulets

Ancient Egyptians used amulets for numerous reasons, and based on archaeological discoveries, the use of amulets was ubiquitous in Ancient Egypt. They were used for protection, in regeneration magic, as part of funerary rites, and much more.

Amulets were never far removed from ancient Egyptian magic. Even the most non-magical seeming of these amulets involved a level of magical practice from the amulet user. The amulet needed to be "activated," and this could only be done when the user recited a spell over the amulet. These spells were often recorded in papyrus, many of which have survived and give us a better understanding of how ancient Egyptians used amulets in their daily lives.

Excavations in Egypt occur almost year-round, and much of what is found is either fragmented or intact amulets. Given the sheer volume of amulets available for scholars and people interested in ancient Egypt and ancient Egyptian magic, most people now categorize amulets as belonging to one of six distinct groupings or types of amulets.

These groupings are:

Amulets of Deities and Sacred Animals

This is a relatively self-evident classification of amulets.

The ancient Egyptian pantheon features over 1000 deities, many (if not all) of which also have a sacred form. Not all of them were represented in amulet form – amulets were used to ask the represented deity for protection or to use their powers to help you achieve your goals.

Amulets in this category we're sometimes elaborate and include the entire figure of the deity being invoked. However, these amulets were often relatively expensive and not accessible to everyone. The solution was to create amulets displaying their sacred animals.

A deity's sacred animal is a representation of themselves as gods. It was believed that if amulets were created in the shape of a given deity's sacred animal or other symbols, that deity would know that you were actually invoking them rather than the animal.

However, the challenge for archaeologists is that determining who each amulet was meant to invoke could often be difficult. There were only so many ancient animals to go around in Ancient Egypt and far too many deities.

Popular amulets like lioness head amulets remain a mystery for scholars. After all, a lioness head amulet could represent Sekhmet. It could also represent other deities, such as Bastet, Tefnut, and even the male deity, Wadjet. The only way to distinguish who a given amulet was meant for was based on engravings and context clues.

Amulets of Protection

Again, the name is relatively self-explanatory. These amulets were meant to shield the bearer from bad luck, providing them with good luck and protecting their life. The scarab is the most popular version of an amulet for protection, and the next section will go into the critical role the scarab played in Egyptian religious life.

Know of Isis.

A unique protection amulet was the Tyet of Isis. Also known as the *knot* (or girdle of Isis), this symbol was linked to the goddess Isis. It looks a lot like an Ankh, but the arms on the side are curved downward instead of sticking straight out. It symbolizes similar things to the Ankh, translating to life and wellbeing. The shape also resembles a knot of cloth. Some suggest that it is a representation of a bandage used to absorb menstrual blood. This amulet was used to protect the dead, and one of the first Tyet amulets was found in a tomb from the First Dynasty.

Scarab Amulets for the Living

Scarabs were an enormously popular type of amulet among the ancient Egyptians, and this popularity continued from the Middle Kingdom through the pharaonic period and beyond. Not only were they used as amulets, but the shape of the scarab was also used as part of both administrative and personal seals and decorative jewelry.

Scarabs were considered a representation of the deity Khepri, who represents the rising sun, creation, and the renewal of life. He was considered an aspect of the sun deity Ra and represented the morning sun (Ra was the midday sun and Atum the evening sun).

Additionally, ancient Egyptians viewed the scarab beetle as a magical creature. This stemmed from a misunderstanding of the beetle's life cycle – adult scarabs lay their eggs in dung balls that are buried underground. To unknowing observers, the hatching of young scarab beetles can be mistaken for them emerging fully formed out of dung, an unlikely and magical event of self-creation. For this reason, the Egyptian term for scarab literally translates to "to come into being."

Furthermore, as part of gathering dung balls in which to lay their eggs, the scarabs roll these balls across the landscape. Egyptians saw this act as similar to the sun's movement from the east to the west.

These two factors caused the young sun god – Khepri – to become undeniably linked to Ancient Egyptian religion. Khepri was a scarab-headed god, and he was thought to be reborn every morning at sunrise in the form of a winged scarab beetle.

Because of the scarab's ability to regenerate and rejuvenate and its links to the sun god, scarab amulets were used as protective amulets for the living. Commemorative scarabs were made by pharaohs and used to commemorate military victories or sent out as diplomatic gifts, and others were found with inscriptions of royal names. Scarabs with royal names inscribed were often created during a pharaoh's rule – the more scarabs with his name found, the longer (and better) he ruled.

Lots of scarabs have been found, and many of those were inscribed with the name of King Tuthmosis III. Many of these date to after his reign – these were likely created due to his worship. All pharaohs were worshiped as gods after death, but popular worship of Tuthmosis III seems to have continued centuries after his relatively rare death. This case was repeated (though in fewer numbers) in the case of Rameses II, Rameses the Great, who is regarded as perhaps the greatest Egyptian Pharaoh (along with the aforementioned Tuthmosis III).

Amulets of Assimilation

Amulets of assimilation are likely to have been the oldest form of amulets. The oldest ones were not physical representations of Egyptian symbols - rather, they were representations of parts of a human or animal body.

These amulets were believed to give the bearer the power represented by the body part.

One of the most important amulets of assimilation was the heart amulet, created to resemble a human heart. Ancient Egyptians believed the heart was the most important of all human organs, and they considered it to be the seat of intelligence - the place from where our feelings, actions, thoughts, and memories originated.

These amulets were placed on the upper torso of every Egyptian mummy - they served as almost a "replacement," ensuring the mummy would have a heart should its mummified heart be destroyed. The heart was the only organ that was left within the body during mummification, as its importance meant that the deceased would require it in the afterlife.

Heart amulets also served as a way to protect a mummy's heart and to ensure that the deceased would be positively received during the Weighing of the Heart.

Amulets of Power

These were amulets that conferred power upon the bearer or represented the bearer's power. These most commonly took the form of royal symbols, such as:

- The red crown
- Uraeus serpent
- Djed pillar

Over time, these amulets were no longer limited to use by royals and those to whom royalty gave the amulets. They were common in ancient Egyptian burials, and many scholars believe they represent the greater access to mummification - where it was once limited to royalty. Over time, it became accessible to everyone.

Other amulets of power included symbols that had innate powers. Bearers believed that using these amulets would transfer the power of the object to them. Amulets of power were representations of generally inanimate objects.

Amulets of Possessions, Offerings, and Property

As the name implies, these amulets were replicas of a person's property and possessions and any offerings they made to the deities or the deceased.

Amulets of property and possessions represented items that would be needed by the deceased in the afterlife and ranged from eating vessels, writing tablets, clothes, beauty materials, and more. These items were also generally present in a person's tomb. However, if grave robbers stole them, the belief was that the amulets would magically transform into the real items, ensuring that the deceased would experience no difficulties in the afterlife.

Amulets of offerings generally took the form of replicas of food offerings. Food offerings were placed outside ancient Egyptian tombs, similar to how we leave offerings on a person's grave today. The belief was that these offerings would be the food and drink that would sustain a person in the afterlife. Occasionally, offerings included other objects, including weapons, combs, and hairpins - anything the deceased's family thought would be useful or desirable in the afterlife.

However, it was the food offerings that were the most important. Because of this, amulets of food offerings were placed in the tomb at the burial. If the deceased's descendants did not present other food offerings, like the amulets of property and possessions, they would magically take on the form of the real item, ensuring the person remained nourished in the afterlife.

One unique amulet in this category was the situla amulet. "Situla" is the Latin word for "bucket" or "pail" and refers to a series of bucket-shaped vessels found in multiple cultures. It was used as part of the daily ceremony in which the deceased was offered food and drink offerings, and, in this case, the situla would have contained water or milk.

However, it was also used in magical rituals, and the situla used during these rituals was believed to contain a liquid with healing properties. Situla amulets were placed on the throats of the deceased, and they were believed to have the same healing powers as the liquid they contained when used in rituals.

Making Your Own Egyptian Amulets

While it is possible to buy pre-made Egyptian amulets, many people prefer to hand-make their magical tools where possible. If this is the case, it is possible for you to make your own Egyptian amulets.

These amulets can be made from various materials, including metal, wood, and faience. The material you choose depends on what you're most comfortable working with. However, out of all the options, the most convenient (and easiest) to use is quick-drying polymer clay.

The first step is to choose a design for your amulet. You'll need to choose an amulet type and symbol that matches what you'll use it for. For example, if you're looking for an amulet of protection, a scarab or Tyet knot are popular choices. Similarly, you might choose a wedjat eye amulet if you are looking for an amulet to help with healing and recovery.

Once you know the shape of the amulet you want, you can move on to actually making your amulet. Here's what you need to do:

Clean a space you can use as a work area.

Place scrap paper over the surface on which you will be working. This will protect the surface from any damage while you make your amulet.

Roll out your clay until you get the desired thickness. You can use your hand for this step.

Sketch the amulet shape onto the clay. If you're good at drawing, you could do this freehand. However, if you're not the greatest artist, you can print out the amulet's design using an inkjet printer with ink meant to bleed when wet. Then, lay the freshly printed image face down on the clay so that the ink is in contact with the clay, and rub the paper to transfer the image to the clay. The print should be in contact with the clay for 30 seconds to 1 minute. When you feel it has transferred, peel a small corner of the paper to see if your guess is right. If it has transferred, you can peel away the full print. If not, let it stay for a few more seconds. Ideally, you should do this with fresh clay, as it will be moist. However, if you do not have access to fresh clay, you can use water to dampen the back of the image when you're rubbing the paper.

Once the design is on the clay, cut it out using a modeling tool. Remove the excess clay and store it away, leaving the amulet to air dry. If the clay you're using isn't an air-drying one, bake it for a few seconds in your oven.

If you want, paint your amulet with acrylic paint, watercolors, or oil paint.

Once the amulet is dry, punch a hole in it and run a string through it if you want to wear it as a necklace, bracelet, or another type of jewelry.

Alternatively, if you're confident in your artistic skills, you could simply sculpt the amulet of your choice with clay and reference images.

Keep in mind that making your own amulets is not a necessity. If you need a more complex design and aren't confident of your artistic abilities, you need a freestanding amulet, and you aren't a sculptor, or you simply don't have the time to make your own can always buy a pre-made amulet. Remember, most ancient Egyptians would have bought their amulets rather than crafting them with their hands. Your amulets won't lose power for having been bought rather than handmade.

How to Cleanse Your Amulet

Cleansing your amulet is a relatively easy process. All you need to do is wash it in a saltwater bath and then pass it through incense smoke. While you do so, visualize all the energies that the amulet or the base materials you used may have accumulated before it reached your hands and took its current shape. Visualize these energies leaving the amulet, disappearing into the universe around you, sinking into the saltwater, or sinking into the ground.

Your amulet is now pure. If you visualize the energies passing into the saltwater, dispose of the saltwater. If not, you can release it into the ocean or the nearest body of water.

How to Set Your Intentions into Your Amulet

In general, you don't need to set intentions into Egyptian amulets. Unlike many modern designs, each Egyptian amulet has its own purpose.

However, there may be occasions when you want to direct the power of your amulet for a specific purpose. You should plan your goal first; then, write it down on a piece of paper, parchment, or papyrus.

Once this is ready, prepare your altar and have a quick ritual bath. Then, you should:

Cleanse the space of negative energy and make a circle around your altar.

Pray to the deities and call the elements while lighting your altar candles.

Cleanse the talisman as described above.

Dress your spell candle.

Read your goal while lighting your spell candle. This will serve as your magical incantation.

Hold the talisman in your hands and repeat the incantation several times, visualizing your goal and visualizing its energy pouring into the talisman.

Pray to the deity of your choice, asking them for their help.

Meditate on your goal.

Place the talisman where it will be kept, or wear it if you will be wearing it on your person.

Thank the deity. This can involve an offering - it's up to you.

Close the circle.

Amulets are not the only ancient Egyptian magical tools you can create. If you want to know about more ancient Egyptian magical tools that you can incorporate into your practice, turn the page and keep reading. In the next chapter, we'll cover tools like the ushabti, sistrum, shendyt, and magic wand to help you understand their history and how you can create them at home (or otherwise find them). We'll also explore how you can make an altar to the deity of your choice.

Chapter 7: More Magical Tools to Create

As mentioned in the previous chapter, amulets are not the only ancient Egyptian magical tools you can access and use today. The ancient Egyptians used several tools and objects considered to be magical or powerful in their own right, and many of these are accessible and usable today.

In this chapter, we'll examine some of these tools. We'll cover their history and look at ways you can access the tools and use them in your magical practice today. We'll also look at ways in which you can create a shrine or altar to a particular Egyptian deity (or deities), so you have a space in your home where you can worship them.

Book of the Dead

The Book of the Dead.
https://commons.wikimedia.org/wiki/File:Book_of_the_dead_egypt.jpg

Perhaps the best-known ancient Egyptian magical tool today is the Book of the Dead. This book wasn't a single canonical book that was replicated. Rather, it is the common name for a collection of funerary texts with spells and magical formulas that were placed in the tomb.

This text was believed to protect the deceased and help them through their journey to the underworld (the Duat). We know of at least 192 spells that were included in the Book of the Dead. There was no single text that contained all the known spells, and they have been collected from different extant examples of the Book of the Dead.

Each spell has a different purpose. For example, some are meant to provide the deceased with mystical knowledge in the afterlife, while others are meant to help with the preservation of different aspects of the deceased's body and personality. Even others are meant to protect the deceased person from forces hostile to them as they make their way through the underworld.

A Book of the Dead was an expensive item. It was produced by scribes, and the cost of a copy could be as much as half of the yearly pay of a laborer. Because of this, copies were generally found in the tombs of the elite, including royalty, officials, scribes, and priests.

How to Make Your own Book of the Dead

The Book of the Dead is one of the ancient Egyptian magical tools that should be bought rather than created. Unless you're skilled at writing hieroglyphics, copying it down is a complicated task, and there's a strong possibility that you will make mistakes.

However, if you are skilled at hieroglyphics, copies of the Book of the Dead are available online, and you can use them as a source to create your own reproduction. The production process is a relatively simple undertaking beyond having knowledge of the symbols. All you need to do is copy them on paper or parchment.

You can use the Book of the Dead as part of your own death and mourning rituals. It can be placed in the grave with a deceased loved one to protect them on their journey to the afterlife or as part of the offerings you leave for them on your altar. You can even leave it as an offering on a loved one's grave or place of burial.

Sekhem Scepter

A sekhem was a ritual scepter used to symbolize power and might. The word "sekhem" was often incorporated into a royal's name, such as Sekhemkhet, a pharaoh from the Old Kingdom.

Royalty and other important officials used it. It was also considered to be a symbol of underworld deities, especially Anubis. It was a sacred object of Anubis's, and the god was frequently shown in a reclining position with the sekhem positioned behind him.

Because of its connection to Anubis, the sekhem was also used during ceremonial offerings to the dead. It was held by the person making an offering in the right hand. Next, it was waved over any offerings to be made, as ritual spells were being cast before the offerings were presented.

The shape of the sekhem had some variations but generally resembled the flat head of a paddle over a long handle.

How to Make Your Own Sekhem

Sekhem scepters can be hard to find online. If you're not very good with your hands, you can get a custom-made one. Alternatively, you can start with a wood flat-headed paddle and carve it down to resemble a scepter.

You can even carve your own from scratch if you are skilled at wood carving.

If none of these options is possible, you can create your own symbolic sekhem. You don't need carving skills for this – simply a block of wood, some paper, and tools to cut wood.

Draw the design of a sekhem on your piece of paper, or trace it from a design you find online. Transfer the design to the block of wood. Then, cut out the shape of the sekhem. You don't need to do much, unlike carving an actual sekhem or cutting a paddle down to shape. While this sekhem will not be perfect, it will be enough.

You can use your sekhem when creating altars for the deceased. Use it when making offerings to loved ones who have passed away, and wave it over an offering as the ancient Egyptians would have done. You should wave it four or five times for each offering.

Crook and Flail

Crook and flail.

Jeff Dahl, CC BY-SA 4.0 <https://creativecommons.org/licenses/by-sa/4.0>, via Wikimedia Commons: https://commons.wikimedia.org/wiki/File:Crook_and_flail.svg

The crook and flail were symbols of royal power in ancient Egypt and were only used by the pharaoh and, in exceedingly rare cases, by other high officials and priests. They held a lot of power and represented the power of the Pharaoh. They were never depicted with the gods.

The only deity that was an exception to this rule was Osiris, as the crook and the flail were originally his symbols that would develop into important signifiers of the pharaoh's rule. The crook was a shepherd's crook and looked similar to a cane with a hooked handle. The flail had three strands of beads attached to a stiff rod. The strands could vary in size, design, and complexity.

How to Make Your Own Crook and Flail

Due to their ubiquity as items carried by pharaohs, the crook and flail are easily purchasable in prop form. However, if you cannot find one in your local store or you prefer to make your own, the process is very simple.

All you'll need is some Christmas ornaments, super glue, and paint (gold and blue).

Take a large plastic ornament candy cane and spray-paint it gold.

Once the paint dries, snap it in half.

Paint blue stripes on each half so that the cane alternates between blue and gold stripes.

Allow the halves to dry.

Put the half with the candy cane head aside. This is your crook.

Take three plastic ornament icicles and spray-paint them gold.

Allow them to dry, and paint blue stripes as you did with the candy cane.

Once the paint dries, use the loop of string attached to them to tie them to the "flail" half of the candy cane. Use super glue to hold them in place.

Let the super glue dry.

Your crook and flail are ready.

You can use your crook and flail as offerings to Osiris or on an altar to the deity when praying to him.

Ushabti Figure

Also known as a shabti, an ushabti figure was a type of small statuette found in Egyptian tombs. Ushabtis were placed in large numbers in graves – the higher the person's status in life, the more ushabti figures they had in their tombs.

These figures were meant to serve as servants and laborers for the deceased in the afterlife, conducting manual tasks on their behalf. Because of this, many of these figurines generally carried farming implements.

How to Make Your Own Ushabti Figure

An ushabti figure is a relatively easy magical tool to make. Almost any human-form figurine can stand in for an ushabti. If you don't already have human-like figurines at home, one easy way to get some is to buy children's dolls.

If you want to make them a bit more formal, you can use the figurine as a starting-off point and then sew clothes for it. This allows you to personalize the figurine by creating different clothes for each figure.

Alternatively, you can also make your ushabti figures out of wood, clay, stone, enamel, faience, metal, glass, or terracotta. You can use any material you're comfortable with - in fact, the earliest ushabtis were made from wax. They were generally made to resemble mummies, so you can also use scrap cloth and draw a human figure.

Like other ancient Egyptian magical grave goods, ushabti figures can be used in altars for the deceased. They can be offered in ways similar to how the ancient Egyptians offered them, as magical figurines that reduced the physical labor expected of the deceased in the afterlife.

Nemes

The nemes was a striped headdress or head cloth used by the pharaohs as a symbol of their power. Though it isn't a crown, its use was limited to pharaohs and Roman emperors. If you've ever seen an image of the mask of Tutankhamun, the nemes is the striped headdress depicted on the mask.

The use of this piece of cloth has evolved over the years. The members of the Hermetic Order of the Golden Dawn used the nemes as part of their ritualistic clothes.

How to Make Your Own Nemes

You can easily find a pattern for a nemes online. Make it out of white or yellow cloth, and paint the stripes with blue paint.

You can use your nemes as ceremonial garb when conducting your rituals. The nemes were also worn by statues of the deities Osiris, Isis, and Nephthys. It can be used to decorate your altars dedicated to these deities.

Sistrum

The sistrum is a musical instrument that was used in dances and religious ceremonies and was often seen with Hathor and Ihy (her son). The handle was modeled after a cow's head, taking up a u-shape that looked like the head and horns. Hathor was generally depicted as a goddess wearing a cow headdress or as a reclining cow, which linked her to the sistrum.

The instrument was used during the flooding of the Nile. It was shaken over the waters of the Nile as a way to frighten Set, the god of disorder and storms. It was also linked to the goddesses Amun, Horus, Bat, Bast, and Isis. It is still used in rituals of the Oriental Orthodox Churches.

How to Make Your Own Sistrum

You can either buy a model of a sistrum or make your own model from clay.

The sistrum can be used to decorate altars to the deities Isis, Amun, Horus, Hathor, Bat, and Bast. You can also use it while performing fertility and weather magic, especially magic associated with rain.

Birth Tusk/Magic Wand

The birth tusk is a magic wand used by the ancient Egyptians when performing protective magic. These wands were originally made with hippopotamus ivory, hence their name. They were occasionally made of wood.

However, hippopotamus ivory was the most common material. This is because the fearsome hippopotamus was thought to help ward off evil. It was used to protect against illnesses and evil spirits and was commonly carried by nurses during childbirth as a way to protect the mother and child.

How to Make Your Own Birth Tusk

You can carve your own birth tusk out of wood. To infuse it with the power of the hippopotamus, carve it with a hippopotamus symbol. It should also be carved with other protective symbols.

The birth tusk/magic wand can be used when performing fertility and protective magic. It can be used in place of your existing wand or in concert with it. You can also use it when performing childbirth rituals as a protective tool.

Shendyt

The shendyt was an Egyptian garment similar to a skirt or a kilt. Men wore it around the waist and reached just above the knees. While commoners usually wore it, it was also worn by officials, royalty, and even pharaohs. Additionally, it was worn by male deities in statutory and artistic representations.

How to Make Your Own Shendyt

You can easily find a pattern for a shendyt online. You can make it out of scrap cloth - linen was the most common fabric used in ancient Egypt, though you can use any other material you have on hand.

You can wear the shendyt when performing ceremonies and rituals.

How to Make an Egyptian Altar

The ancient Egyptians made offerings to the deities on altars located outside the main sanctuary of a temple dedicated to that deity. They were also placed in royal courts and in the homes of worshippers.

To make your own altar, you will need the following:

- Representations of the four elements
- Offerings to the deity to whom you are making an altar
- A focal point - a symbol of the deity would be a good option
- The magical tools you will be using
- Egyptian symbols and amulets

To make the altar, you will need a table or any other flat surface. Place each representation of the elements on each of the corners of the table.

Cover the table with a cloth decorated with ancient Egyptian symbols. You can paint these on or transfer them to the cloth with stickers.

Once your altar is dressed, place your focal point in the center of the altar, and place the amulets around the altar. Start an offering ritual, and place your offerings on the altar to the deity.

You can use this altar to worship the deity, perform your regular rituals, or use it in concert with any other altars you have set up. People often set up at least two rituals - one dedicated to the deity of their choice and the other to the ancestors and the deceased.

Magical tools can also be used in other ways, such as when performing divination magic and plant magic. This book will explain how to perform ancient Egyptian divination and plant magic. The next chapter will cover divination magic in detail, while the chapter after that will explore sacred plant and herb magic.

We'll also explore spells and rituals you can perform using your magical tools. This will include spells and rituals for a variety of purposes, including protection magic, healing magic, and love magic. Later in this book, you'll find step-by-step instructions on performing each ritual from start to finish.

By the end, you'll know how to use all your tools and amulets to their fullest extent. You'll have a better understanding of ancient Egyptian magic and be ready to incorporate it into your regular rituals and magic practice.

Chapter 8: Methods of Divination

The most well-documented method of divination in ancient Egypt was scrying, although there are records of several other techniques used around that time. Oil scrying, moon divination, and dream interpretation are just some of the most common methods ancient Egyptians used to reveal fate. This chapter discusses these techniques and how divination was perceived in ancient Egypt. You'll also be provided with several techniques you, as a contemporary practitioner, can incorporate into your divinatory practices. To help you get the most out of any technique, it's recommended that you also use grounding, cleansing, and protection rituals as part of your preparation process.

Divination in Ancient Egypt

Unlike in modern practices (where divination is often used for self-exploration), in ancient Egypt, the primary focus of divinatory practices was to find answers about present situations. Practitioners would try to obtain all the valuable information they could get about the present. They would then use this information to change their behavior, which, in turn, had the power to change future outcomes. In more challenging situations, they would ask a deity for answers and guidance, compelling them to help the practitioners make the desired changes.

Some of the ways the art of divination was used in ancient Egypt (and can still be used) was to find answers, and items, reconnect with people, and predict the future using dreams, omens, and visions. That is to predict possible outcomes of future events and situations, not exactly how things will happen. Even ancient Egyptians knew divination couldn't give a practitioner direct answers. It would only guide them toward the most desirable path.

Preparatory Rituals

How well you predict the outcome of future events depends on how much you practice doing it and how you prepare for it. Because you'll be tapping into powerful energy sources and receiving messages you'll need to interpret correctly, you must take a few safety measures before delving into divinatory practices.

Grounding Ritual

The first step is to perform a grounding meditation to prepare your mind, body, and soul for focusing on your intent and receiving the messages. There are many ways to do this, including the ever-popular root rituals often recommended for beginners. Here is a simple grounding root ritual you can perform:

Sit in a comfortable position with your feet planted firmly on the ground.

Slowing your breath, bring your awareness to your feet, and feel the ground beneath them.

Close your eyes and visualize natural energy taking the form of roots around your feet and traveling up your legs by growing roots.

Imagine the roots growing longer and stronger, holding you firmly in place.

Let this centered state relax you, and when it does, open your eyes.

Protection Ritual

The next step is to perform a protection spell to keep the negative influences away during your divinatory ritual. A great way for beginners to protect themselves is through a visualization technique which requires very few tools. In fact, you don't even have to use anything other than your imagination for the following method. If you want to use anything else, you can choose something as simple as a black candle, a picture of a black cat, or black and white crystals. Here is how to perform this protection ritual:

Start by relaxing your mind and body through deep breathing or a simple meditation technique.

Next, visualize a bright orb of light emerging at your feet and enveloping your entire body. Feel free to make the orb any color or shape you like, using your imagination.

Imagine the orb slowly filling your body with protective energy. Feel how it's reassuring you and letting you know that you will be safe spiritually during the divination ritual and that no negative energy will be able to harm you.

Finish the ritual with positive affirmations as a further reminder of your strength and power. The more confident you are in your ability to protect yourself, your shield will become stronger.

Cleansing Your Tools, Space, and Body

You should also think about cleansing your space, your tools, and yourself from any negative energy that may influence your results. When it comes to energetically cleansing your tools, the method you use depends on the type of tools you need to purify. Clear stones, crystal balls, water, mirrors, and other shining surfaces used for scrying are typically cleansed by being left out under the moonlight overnight. Other tools can be cleaned by passing them over the smoke of a black or white candle or the incense of your choice.

The latter method also applies to the divination space you'll use. Divinatory practices are commonly performed in an open space under the moon's protection during the night. So, if you opt for this method, nature will take care of shielding your sacred space. However, depending on how strictly you want to follow the ancient Egyptian traditions, your primary concern should be purifying your body. According to the ancient practice, a person set to perform divination had to undergo a 3-day cleansing process. This meant abstaining from unhealthy vices and behavior (including the use of alcohol), eating food that promoted purification, and taking cleansing baths.

Preparing Your Space

Preparing your space will help you set the appropriate mood for your divinatory ritual. The amount of natural light you have in your sacred space while performing divination will affect your mood and your ability to interpret the messages you'll receive. This light can come from candles (if you are performing the ritual indoors), the sun (which can be used both outdoors and indoors), or the moon (typically used for night scrying). Apart from the specific divination method you opt for, the amount of light will also depend on your preferences. It's okay if you don't know how much you'll need, as you'll figure it out as you practice.

The same goes for the ambient sound. Some practitioners prefer silence when looking for answers, while others use music to relax and reach a trance-like state. Certain essential oil and incense can also help you set the perfect mood for a relaxing session. Herbs were commonly used for similar purposes used by ancient Egyptians.

Regardless of how you prepare for a divination ritual, the space you choose for it must be away from all the distractions of the modern world. All electronic devices should be turned off (you can put your phone in flight mode), and any artificial lights should be turned off. You may also want to prepare a pen and a piece of paper in case you want to write down the answers so you can analyze them later. This will be particularly helpful if you are new to divination techniques or are performing dream divination.

Common Divinatory Methods in Ancient Egypt

The primary divinatory methods used in ancient Egypt were trance, water, and oil scrying, fire messages, divination via knots, and dream interpretation. Here are how these methods worked in ancient Egypt and how you can perform them today.

Dream Divination

The ancient Egyptians believed that dreams had the power to convey messages from the spiritual world, which is why they used dream interpretation as a common divination method. If you want the future to reveal itself through your dreams, you should address a specific guide from which you want to receive the answers. They'll visit you in your sleep and convey messages you'll interpret when you awake. Here is how to do this method:

Prepare for sleep with your preferred relaxation method by removing all distractions like light and sound sources.

Light a black candle and say a prayer to your guide, asking them for the answers you seek about your future.

Make sure you thank them for any messages they send and, if you wish, prepare a small offering.

Leave a piece of paper and a pen at your bedside and go to bed without using any electronic device.

You may wake right after receiving a message from the spiritual world, in which case, you write down what you saw right away.

Even if you don't wake up right away, you may still want to record the messages in the morning, even if you know what they mean. This can serve you as a reference for future divinatory practices.

Using Knots for Divination

The use of knots in witchcraft originated in Ancient Egypt, and there is evidence that knots were often employed for divination purposes. This typically involved making an amulet from the knots and using it for interpretation. With the following method, you can also perform a quick divinatory ritual:

Find 16 individual, foot-long threads - 4 white, 4 red, 4 blue, and 4 green ones.

Gather the threads into one band and stain the band with a drop of red coloring. Traditionally the practitioner's blood was used for staining, but any red color will do.

Bind the band around your wrists, get into a relaxed state and focus on the question you want to be answered.

The band will act as a vessel for the messages, so focus on your hand when expecting the answers.

Visualize the messages in the form of energy traveling from your arm toward your body and head.

Once they reach your mind, it will be up to you to interpret them.

Moon Divination

The ancient Egyptians acknowledged the moon's influence on human life in both a physical and a spiritual sense. They believed that the full moon enhanced the impact of whatever actions you took, and it reflected your intentions perfectly. Because of this, they were more than ready to use the reflection of the moon for divinatory purposes, and such is the case with the following method:

Start by finding a place where you'll perform the ritual outdoors at the full moon. If you can't go outside, stand by an open window where the moon shines in, and you can see its likeness.

Gather a bowl of water, incense, and a censer for holding the burning incense.

Take the items from above to the place you've chosen for divination.

Place the incense in the censer on the ground and stand straight, holding the bowl of water. Stand in a position where you can see the moon's reflection on the water's surface.

Recite the following invocation 7-9 times, either in your mind or aloud, depending on what helps you focus more:

"For you, great Moon, the leader of the stars,

you who helped form them,

listen now to what I have to say.

Follow the words of my mouth, and reveal your secrets to me!"

Now, carefully consider anything you may hear, see, or otherwise perceive. If you are lucky, the Moon goddess herself will appear and present you with the answers to your question.

You may also receive other signs, such as the movement in the water or the appearance of a key part of your answer on the moon's surface.

Oil Scrying

Another common form of divination in ancient Egypt involved the use of an oil lamp. Lamps used for divination were typically white, free from any red colors, and lit in dark, serious places. Later on, this was replaced by the use of oil scrying, which is essentially the combination of water scrying and the oil lamp method. Just as lamps were forbidden to touch the ground, it's recommended not to place any vessel with oil onto the ground. The steps for this method are similar to the moon scrying technique, except you'll be using vegetable oil. Unlike water, oil doesn't break the image, so you'll be able to focus for longer. Make sure you pour the oil into the bowl very slowly to prevent it from becoming cloudy, as this will hinder your ability to interpret spiritual messages.

Additional Tips for Divination

Whether it's part of ancient Egyptian or any other magic practice, divination is a skill that requires a lot of practice to master. That said, there are a few ways to advance your learning journey. Starting by setting a broad intention, no matter how tempting it is, it is recommended to seek a direct answer. It's more than likely that you will not receive one even after plenty of practice as a beginner, but you won't even notice whether you do or not. Remember, you will experience things you've never seen before, which makes interpreting any message challenging, not to mention that you can't be sure in which form the response will come. Setting a specific intention will not give you a specific answer - and can even block messages that may hold the answer you seek.

For example, you can set an intention like this:

"My mind and heart are now open to any messages that guide me toward my future goal."

An intention like this communicates that you want positive or constructive messages regarding your current life but are open to whatever form you may receive them. Once you practice scrying a little more, you get more familiar with the type of message you receive, and you learn how to interpret them. Then you can move on to asking for answers to more specific issues. However, you still can't ask direct questions, as the answers will not be direct either. An example of a more specific intention could be:

"My mind and heart are now open to receiving any messages regarding my current financial status."

Deep breathing can help you achieve and maintain the perfect focus - and if it doesn't, you can still do a few things to maintain concentration. With some methods, you can close your eyes to close out any visual distractions, whereas, with others (like with scrying), you'll need to keep your eyes unfocused, allowing your mind to focus instead. You can do this by softening your gaze.

Once the focus is transferred to your mind's eye, you may begin to see symbols, shapes, or even living beings appear. Keep in mind that it may take 5-10 minutes of gazing before anything appears, so make sure you wait at least that long. Don't second guess what you see - even if it seems that what you have seen, heard, or otherwise perceived was the product of your imagination. It's more likely that the gut feeling you got was right, no matter how random it may seem, and it turns out to be a message you'll benefit from later on.

Since you'll probably be in a deep meditative state while performing divination, your conscious mind may need a little help to remember what you've experienced. It's recommended to keep a journal in which you record your experience. When scrying, make sure you do this after the session, so you don't have to look away from the surface. Apart from writing it down, you can also record your session using your phone to ensure you don't miss out on any part of the message. If you are going to do this, practice describing every part of your experience aloud. This way, you'll know what you are listening to when you replay the recording.

Chapter 9: Sacred Plants and Herbs

Another form of magical practice which originated in ancient Egypt is plant magic. Egyptians used sacred plants and herbs for healing rites, love spells, self-empowerment rituals, and tools for warding off negative influences. They believed that each plant has its own magical effect, and knowing the strengths of a specific plant is key to successfully using them in spellwork. Because of this, herbs can enhance your practice, even if you don't have too much experience. Plant magic will always have the desired result. You just have to know how to employ it correctly.

The magic within the plants, and the speed with which they act, allow you to use them more efficiently than any other magical art form. When casting a spell, you find the plants or herbs that possess the properties you want to incorporate into your work, and your spell will be instantly empowered with natural magic. This chapter contains an extensive list of powerful plants and herbs used in ancient Egyptian spell work and their spiritual meaning and magical purposes.

Ancient Egyptian Herbs and Plants

Acacia

You'll recognize Acacia trees by their characteristic thorns, segmented leaves, and pea-like legumes. In ancient times, Egyptians associated

Acacia with deities like Ra, Diana, Osiris, and Astarte - all known for being aligned with powerful elements such as the air or the sun itself. It's believed that Acacia carries distinctively masculine energy, which is why it's often used for protection spells and for drawing psychic energy for powerful spellwork.

As a beginner, you can use Acacia to enrich your practice by incorporating them into your ritual while you are still learning. One way to use this is to extract the gum from the tree by cutting the branch and simply letting it drip out, making it a base for your favorite incense. You can also combine the plant with sandalwood and make a relaxing incense you use during your preparatory meditation. If you want to reach out to a soul inhabiting the spiritual world or use your power more confidently, you should burn Acacia leaves on charcoal while focusing on your intention.

African Violet

For the ancient Egyptians, African Violet represented the feminine counterpart of Acacia's masculine energy. Its power is said to be aligned with the energy of Venus and the water element. This small plant is known for its round leaves and bright or deep purple flowers.

You may use it for spiritual protection during spellwork or simply to enhance your spirituality and those who live in your home. Remember that, unlike other violet varieties, African Violet isn't an edible plant. In fact, its flowers can be highly toxic for pets and small children, so make sure to keep them away from them and avoid ingesting them.

Catnip

Catnip was used to attract good luck in cat magic.
Robert Flogaus-Faust, CC BY 4.0 <https://creativecommons.org/licenses/by/4.0>, via
Wikimedia Commons: https://commons.wikimedia.org/wiki/File:Nepeta_cataria_3_RF.jpg

Due to their fascination with cat magic, ancient Egyptians made many magical associations with these four-legged creatures. One of these was the use of catnip in cat magic, which was typically performed to attract good luck and benevolent spirits. It has small purple flowers and leaves similar to mint. You can use it to enhance happiness and promote beauty. You can hang it in a satchel above head level to induce beauty and happiness. Another great way to use catnip satchels is in conjunction with rose petals. Mix these two, scoop up some of the mixture into your hands, and let it warm up. After that, you should hold someone else's hand. This person will become one of your best friends. While catnip can be beneficial for cats in some quantities, it can be toxic in high doses.

Chamomile

Chamomile is one of the most ancient herbs used in healing magic. Due to its delicate yet bright white flower, ancient Egyptians associated this plant with the sun's deities. It was often used to invoke the god Ra for its healing powers when they needed remedies for communicable diseases like malaria. Ancient Egyptians also used chamomile for mummification because they believed it could help protect the deceased from malicious spirits brought on by insects. Dried plants were added to the bath for relaxation and cleansing before rituals and spell work.

In ancient times, practitioners would even plant chamomile alongside other, more sensitive plants they needed for their work. This ensures the other plant gets all the nutrients needed to thrive. Chamomile is believed to attract wealth and prosperity because fresh plants smell like green apples - and green is the color associated with wealth and material gains. Brew a strong chamomile tea and wash your hands in it before you perform any spell work related to money, work progress, etc. You can also drink a milder version of the tea or place loose dried flowers under your pillow for vision-inducing dream work.

Cinnamon

Also known as sweet wood, cinnamon was another plant used in ancient Egyptian healing and protective magic practices. They used cinnamon oil in beauty rituals, rites for healing scars, enhancing spirituality and psychic abilities, and as part of the concoction used for the mummification process. They also incorporated cinnamon oil and bark into protection and love spell work.

While nowadays, it's typically used for the tantalizing aroma it adds to foods, cinnamon can still find its way into modern spellwork. You can use both the bark and the oil to strengthen love bonds and familial relationships. The oil can also serve as an empowering anointment for candles used during rituals, spells, and meditative practice to enhance your spiritual and psychic powers.

Cypress

Cypress is an evergreen tree known for its longevity, which is why in ancient Egypt, it was considered a symbol of eternity, and it was even said to grant immortality. Its wood was used to make sarcophagi and in various rituals to prolong life. Cypress oil was incorporated into healing magic or spellwork to ward off evil spirits during rituals and ceremonies.

You can also find cypress oil and use this to protect yourself and your work. Its aroma has a comforting effect, which will help you relax and focus on manifesting your intent. Taking a small twig of cypress to the grave of your loved ones will let them know that they are still loved, which will help both of you to move on.

Daisy

Daisies are known for their dainty white flowers and yellow seedbeds. In ancient Egypt, the flowers represented femininity and were also associated with the sun and the water element. Daisies were often offered to female deities when asked for guidance. They were used for divinatory practices and love spells, giving way to modern acts, such as the "love me, love me, not" divination.

You can also use dried flowers to offer to the deity of your choice, scatter them around for love spells, or put them under the loved one's bed. Be careful when doing this, as some people are allergic to daisies. Don't ingest any part of the plant either, nor should you let small children or animals eat them. Several toxic substances lead to vomiting, nausea, and other digestion issues.

Dandelion

Like chamomile, dandelion was also associated with sun deities due to how much young flowers resemble this heavenly body. Its main flower consists of a large group of small needle-like individual flowers. These become translucent when they mature and are easily blown away by the wind and the seeds. Because of this, Egyptians associated dandelions with the air element and believed the tiny flowers to be able to carry messages across this world and the spiritual one.

Nowadays, people use mature flower heads to make a wish before blowing off the seeds, but this can also be used in magical practice. For example, you can do this if you are trying to get a deity to work with you. Or you can simply offer dried younger flowers to the sun gods. Tea made from dandelion roots can also be used in healing magic, whereas tea made from flowers will enhance your psychic abilities and enable spiritual communication.

Elder

The Elder was considered a very powerful source of magic in ancient Egypt. Its flowers have five petals (and the same number of sepals), forming a tiny green star when they come together. Since the number 5 was associated with many mystical happenings, Elderflower was used for a broad range of magical acts. This included spellwork and rituals to find a connection to the natural kingdom, crossing the gateway to the spiritual realm, and healing magic. They may also have used it to represent life's cycle and to celebrate new beginnings after a meaningful period had come to an end. Elder trees were sometimes planted near graves to keep away the evil spirit.

You can nowadays use Elder flowers and bark for protection, grounding, and meditative relaxation, and incorporate these into your practice in several ways. Elder is said to open the mind, so you become open to different kinds of spiritual messages and see things in a more positive light. This can also be helpful in magic meant to heal emotional traumas and open the heart while ensuring it's shielded from further trauma. If you have a larger garden, you can even grow an Elder tree, as it will protect you and your property from harm and bad luck. Berries and mature leaves can be harvested and hung up on doorways for spiritual protection or warding off evil intent sent your way.

Henbane

Recognizable for its large white flowers and green leaves sporting deep white veins, henbane is a plant with powerful properties. Ancient Egyptians used this plant's leaves, flowers, and seeds for healing magic meant to treat mortal injuries. They praised this plant for its pain-relieving effects, which we know results from a compound that relaxes the nervous system. Beginning from the times of the ancient Egyptians, henbane was also one of the ingredients of flying ointment, an incredibly powerful magical tool.

Nowadays, henbane is only recommended to use in healing rituals when you want to invoke spiritual protection for someone who is ill or injured. Don't ingest the plant, as it's extremely toxic and can lead to respiratory and heart issues, even in small amounts. With children and animals, ingesting this plant can have dire consequences.

Lavender

Lavender is known for its fragrant flowers, often used for refreshing the contents of wardrobes, as a relaxation tool, or as an ingredient in natural hygiene products. The ancient Egyptians had similar uses for lavender, as they incorporated it into various aromatherapy treatments and even the mummification process. Lavender was also recorded as a great pain reliever and anti-inflammatory agent to treat burns and wounds. Egyptians included lavender in their magic spells when trying to find a solution for insomnia, indigestion, and many other ailments and symptoms.

In modern times, you can also place dried lavender under your pillow to have a more relaxed sleep. You'll either process messages you receive during the day or find them through dream divination. The calming effect of lavender promotes self-acceptance and harmony. Lavender ashes are a great cleanser that you can use during your preparatory practices. Scattering these ashes around or creating them before your spellwork will ward off malicious influences and the evil spirits themselves. You can also hand a branch of flowers outside your home for added protection.

Lotus

In ancient Egypt, the lotus was believed to have beneficial powers for protection and love. At that time, this plant was viewed as a symbol of spiritual life; according to some sources, it may even have been considered a gateway to the center of the universe. Ancient Egyptians used this plant as an offering to the gods during religious and magic ceremonies. Lotus oil was a traditional wedding gift for the newlyweds as it was believed to help grow and protect their love.

Nowadays, lotus oil can be used in love magic spells, spiritual relaxation, and self-love. Its relaxing aroma can help you become more confident in your abilities, especially in psychic divination. It also promotes spiritual growth and cleansing, truth revelations, and the finding of good luck. You may also use it to calm your mind and during a dream divination session.

Mint

Mint is known for its green, aromatic leaves, which are often used for teas and to enhance the flavor of meals. However, ancient Egyptians often used mint in spells and rituals to encourage love, wealth, and prosperity. Also, mint was believed to help keep out evil spirits and empower practitioners spiritually. It was also used in healing magic to relieve muscle fatigue and digestion issues, just as it's still used today in modern aromatherapy practices.

A cup of mint tea in the morning can bring you good fortune throughout your day, so feel free to drink it anytime you feel down on your luck. Dry out the leaves, and place them over the bed of a person who is ill or injured, and it will ward off negative energy and allow the person to recoup. You can also place dry mint leaves under your pillow before going to sleep. It will provide protection during dream divination. Its relaxing aroma will also enhance your ability to interpret the messages you receive during your sleep.

Mugwort

Mugwort is a herb that promotes psychic development and the enrichment of divinatory practices, particularly during sleep. This plant was also used in ancient Egypt to protect against evil spirits and physical injuries. Due to its ability to neutralize poisons, mugwort was part of Egyptian healing magic practice. It's also recorded to have been used to relieve digestive issues.

In modern times, practitioners use mugwort mainly as a tea prepared to get in the mood for receiving psychic visions, divinatory messages, and prophetic dreams. Dried mugwort can also be smoked or incorporated into ointments and applied to the skin. Depending on the dosage, these applications can help varying degrees of psychoactive effects. Bear in mind that, for this reason, you have to be careful with the dosage and shouldn't let animals or children consume it.

Myrtle

Known for its sweet pink flowers, myrtle was considered one of the greatest tools for love magic in ancient Egypt. Practitioners who wanted to enact a love spell and strengthen their bond with their partner would wear a wreath made of fresh myrtle flowers during the spell. This tree was also associated with fertility and was employed in spells that either encouraged conception or ensured it wouldn't happen quickly (hence why many new brides wear it during their wedding day).

If you want to keep your love life exciting, you can also wear a myrtle wreath. You can give small flower branches to people you want to become friends with. To maintain a youthful appearance and agility, you should drink myrtle tea for 3 days in a row. Growing myrtle in your yard will help you attract wealth, fertile ideas, and new opportunities through which you can persevere.

Rosemary

Like lavender, rosemary is also an incredibly aromatic herb with multiple magical and non-magical properties. It's recognizable for its small spiky leaves that sit on strong branches. Apart from its ability to enhance flavors in the kitchen as a dried loose herb, rosemary is also used in oil infusion form to relieve aches. In ancient Egypt, rosemary was an inevitable part of love spells, was considered an aphrodisiac and protection rites, and was also favored for its cleansing abilities. You can burn rosemary leaves to purify your space and body before spellwork. Placed in a bath, rosemary has a spiritually invigorating effect and will help you chase away negative thoughts. Placing rosemary in a sachet near the entrance of your loved one's home will fortify your relationship, leaving no place for jealousy and mistrust. You can also place rosemary under their pillow to make them think of you more often. Or you can put it under your pillow for deeper relaxation during sleep, enhancing dream visions and warding off nightmare-inducing influences.

Sage

According to ancient Egyptian lore, sage can help ward off evil and was often used in cleansing and other magical ceremonies. Sage has grayish-green juicy leaves, which were dried and either used as a loose herb or burned as part of a smudging ritual. It was said to bring good luck and even help gather the wisdom needed for successful spellwork. Egyptian healing magic has also seen its benefits, as it was often used for its anti-inflammatory properties and to empower one's mind, body, and spirit to help overcome illnesses and injuries.

Apart from adding a great aroma to your dishes, you can also incorporate sage into your own contemporary Egyptian spellwork. You can use it for smudging or simply burn it as incense during preparatory or meditative practices. It will help you overcome grief and traumatic events and build up your emotional and spiritual strength. Use it in your cleansing ceremonies to add purity, especially to your spirit, and to rid yourself and your space of negative spirits and energies. Burning sage is generally recommended if you are new to magical practices and are looking for quick and easy ways to eliminate negative influences that can hinder your learning journey.

Vervain

Vervain is another plant with both cleansing and protective properties. In ancient Egypt, it was used to purify a sacred ritual space and to ensure that all those who cast the spell were protected from evil influences. There is also evidence that it was used in healing magic and was said to be particularly effective for digestive and kidney issues.

You can dry its purple flowers and sprinkle them around your home and ritual site to keep away evil spirits. You can also prepare tea from the loose vervain herbs to soothe your digestive system or use this brew for magical purposes. Drink it before your divination practice or astral work, and your ability to interpret spiritual messages will increase. You can also juice the fresh plant and incorporate it into love spells and potions. It will also enhance your psychic abilities, but be careful with the dosage, as too much of it can cause hallucinations.

Chapter 10: Ancient Egyptian Spells and Rituals

In this chapter, you will find a few Egyptian spells for various purposes like protection, love, abundance, and healing. Keep in mind that this is just one way you can perform these spells. They can be altered in any way you see fit. You'll find step-by-step instructions for different forms of spells, rituals, prayers, and baths.

Spell for Protecting Against Food Poisoning

In Ancient Egypt, food poisoning was believed to have been caused by enemies. If someone suspected that their food was poisoned, they would perform a ritual before eating. The spell was based on the principle of retribution and turned the curse on whoever cast the spell in the first place. To perform this spell, you need to say the following before eating:

"O Sakhmet of yesterday, Widget of today,

You came and replenished my table,

Just as you did for your father when you came forth from the cult city of Pe.

Protect us with that papyrus wand of life, which is in your hand,

In that name of yours of Wadjet.

Shoot your arrow against all the food of him who shall speak against me

By means of any evil matters.

Let a slaughter be made of them like the time when you overpowered the enemies of Re in the primordial age, in the name of your of Sakhmet.

Your offerings belong to me."

You can now eat your food without any fear of poisoning. This spell was also meant to give you a long life by protecting you from any harm that could have been intended by your enemies.

Love Spell

When it comes to love spells, the caster needs to burn different types of offerings in the bathhouse and write the following on the walls:

"I adjure you, earth and waters, by the demon who dwells on you and (I adjure) the fortune of this bath so that, as you blaze and burn and flame, so burn her (the woman targeted) whom (the mother of the woman targeted) bore until she comes to me..."

You also need to include the names of the gods and magical words you will recite when you perform your spell. The spell also includes the following words:

"Holy names, inflame in this way and burn the heart of her..."

If you cast this spell to get someone to fall in love with you, you continue to say this until they do. If you are casting a spell on behalf of someone else, the person who is the focus of the ritual will eventually fall in love with them.

Another love spell to win her involves rubbing a tick from a dead dog onto your loins. This is a simple spell but is believed to be effective. Once a tick bites something, it does not fall away easily unless it is pulled or killed by an insecticide. This would symbolize your new relationship with the person you love.

Protection Spells

Negative energy, angry gods, spiteful demons, spirits, and other magic users can cause bad luck, misfortune, sickness, and many other ailments and accidents. Magic offered a defense mechanism against these ills. Several spells were performed using magical implements, special foodstuffs, talismans, and figurines. Hippo tusks were used to carve magic knives that were specifically intended to protect the children against spells and other dangers that could cause them harm, like snakes. Hippo talismans were very popular since they possessed potent power that could protect the young ones in particular.

Ivory wands were also used to provide a protective circle around the place where a woman would give birth or nurse her child. The wands were inscribed with the dangerous beings that the magician invoked to protect the mother and child. They were portrayed as strangling, stabbing, or biting evil forces that foreigners or snakes represented.

Shouting, stamping, and making a loud noise with drums, rattles, and tambourines were also believed to drive away hostile forces that could cause harm to vulnerable women. Pregnant women and children were also at risk of being attacked by dark forces and needed protection. That's where this spell came in handy.

Amulets have long been used for protection and are shaped like or engraved with depictions of animals and gods. They can also be inscribed with symbols and words to add power and enhance a spell – different animals/gods/royals will provide different types of protection and enhancements. However, if your spell was bent on causing harm to someone, the god rejected it. Therefore, you had to define your intention to avoid tempting the gods. All intentions were supposed to be valid for effective results.

Magical Healing

Different types of diseases were believed to have been caused by spirits, so healing was treated as magical science. Administration of medicines and nursing care were usually accompanied by specific rituals meant to eliminate the pathogenic agents responsible for causing the illness. When children suffered illnesses believed to be caused by evil spirits, the powers of the great god would be invoked by the high priest, and the patient would suddenly become well. Magicians, priests, and physicians all believed in magical powers.

You can attract demons to yourself when bad energy or negative things surround you. Spells can be used to get rid of negativity or evil spirits once they have arrived. Dung was long used in Ancient Egypt to draw out the demon from the body, but honey is also good for warding off evil (and it is not as messy as dung). Images of the evil spirit can be drawn and then destroyed to ward off evil or consume its power so that it becomes powerless. Inscribing healing and protective spells on amulets and statues was another spell performed by the healers.

Several spells included speeches that were recited by a doctor or the patient. Healing was to follow strict guidelines, and the body was supposed to be examined in a certain way. The results were to be interpreted first before treatments were performed. In each organ of the body, there are vessels, and magicians or priests would lay their fingers on the patient to feel the pulse of the heart.

Remedy for Headache

When someone suffered from a terrible headache, a certain spell was performed to address the situation. To perform this, one was supposed to obtain seven threads from a garment, which were made into seven knots. These knots were placed on the left foot of the sick person. The spell caster would recite the following words.

"My head, my head," said Horus.

"The half of my head (= migraine), the half of my head," said Thoth.

"Act for me, mother Isis and Aunt Nephthys!

Give me your head in exchange for my head, the half of my head!"

(Isis speaks): "Just as I have seen these people (= human sufferers), so = I have heard these gods (Horus and Thoth) saying to me on behalf of my son Horus.

'Let there be brought to me your head in exchange for my head.'

You should indicate your gratitude about how the threads brought from the edge of the garment will cure the headache. When word of the issues reaches the gods, a cure will be found.

Magic for Snake Bite

A snake bite often puts the patient's life in danger, and Sekhmet would threaten to cause consequences to the fabric of the world for the curse of the snake bite. He would recite the following prayer to ask for healing.

"The sun barque is at rest and does not proceed,

The sun is still in the same spot as yesterday.

The nourishment is without a ship; the temple is barred,

There the disease will turn back the disturbance

To yesterday's location."

This prayer was meant to protect the patient by blocking any potential harm that could lead to loss of life. The spirits would block the effects of the dark spirits to protect a life.

Daily Worship

Daily worship of the god and goddesses was another crucial ritual performed in places of worship. Each temple was dedicated to a god or goddess, and the Egyptians believed temples were sacred since the gods or goddesses lived there. Because of this, only priests were allowed to enter the temples to make rituals consisting of food offerings, drinks, and clothing to honor and appease the gods. Farmers would bring portions of their harvest to the temple to honor the deities. Every aspect of life in ancient Egypt was based on the beliefs and power of the gods.

Daily Offering Ritual

A daily offering ritual was meant to please the gods and goddesses and ask for protection. This ritual is still relevant today, and it consists of different steps you should follow if you want to perform it. The first step you should take is to burn incense before visiting your shrine. Open the shrine that is usually sealed by a cord. Remove the cord that is tied around the door knobs.

The individual performing the ritual must bow in front of the picture of the deity. They should kiss the ground, and this gesture is followed by raising arms while singing the ideal hymn for the ritual. This is followed by the offerings of scented oil and incense. When you visit the inner shrine, you must repeat the previous stages.

The main offering of the goddess is performed inside the shrine. Wrap the image of the god using four lengths of cloth; each must have a different name. You must provide your image with scented oil, black (lead), and green (copper) eyepaint. When you finish performing the ritual, you should leave the shrine. Make sure you sweep away your footprints and offer incense, natron, and water.

This is a daily offering ritual; you can perform it even if there are no issues you want to solve. It is meant to appease the gods and goddesses, so they continue protecting you against evil spells. When the gods are happy, you will get blessings, making your life much more enjoyable.

Preparations for Spells and Rituals

For magic spells to succeed, specific preparations were necessary, and it was a good idea to avoid unlucky days. Depending on the ritual you want to perform, you must choose the appropriate day, time, and place to do it. In ancient Egypt, most rituals were performed at dawn or dusk, and they were done in dark places and specifically designed for such spiritual endeavors. The magician, ingredients, and medium chosen for failure to uphold a high purity level meant that your ritual could not succeed. If the moon was used as the medium, then it was supposed to be pure. Ingredients and other implements used in the ritual had to be properly cleaned. Before going to the dark chamber for your spell, you had to sprinkle it with clean sand obtained from the great river. A clean vessel of pottery or bronze cup was used to hold pure water that would be used for the ritual.

Magic was an integral component of life in ancient Egypt, and it was used for protection, healing, birth, love, and even death. The gods performed their duties through heka (magic). The power of the gods was used to maintain balance and harmony in the universe. Different forms of magic were performed using various ingredients.

To the ordinary person, magic could be dangerous, and coming into contact with the tools used could be deadly. For instance, accidentally touching the scepter used by the magicians had to be resolved by invoking the king's spell.

Ancient Egyptian Deities A-Z

Egyptian gods family tree.

A

A'ah

A god of the moon. Once called Iah and later called Knonsu.

Aken

Protected the souls of those who traveled by boat to the afterlife.

Aker

Custodian of the horizon from east to west.

Am-Heh

A god from the underworld who lived in a fiery lake.

Amenet

She supplied the dead with food and drink.

Ammit

Her hindquarters were that of a hippo, she had the body of a leopard, and her head was a crocodile.

Amun

The god of the sun and the air. He is the most popular and famous god in the ancient Egyptian Pantheon.

Amenhotep

The god of wisdom and healing.

Amunet

The wife of Amun.

Anat

The Female deity of love, sexuality, fertility, and war.

Anta

The Mother Goddess, often a part of Mut in some form.

Andjety

A god of fertility.

Anhur

The god of war.

Anqet

A part of the Nile river and also associated with fertility.

Anti

The hawk god of upper Egypt.

Anubis

Deity of the deceased.

Anuke

One of the oldest deities of the pantheon. She is the goddess of war.

Apedemak

Another war god who took the form of a lion.

Apep

The serpent demon of chaos.

Apis

The bull-shaped god of fertility.

Arensnuphis

Nubian god and Isis' companion.

Asclepius

The Greek god of healing – who was also worshiped by ancient Egyptians.

Ash

God of the Oases.

Astarte

Goddess of sexuality and fertility.

Aten

The sun deity and the personification of the sun disk.

Atum

The supreme lord of all gods. He is also the god of the sun.

Auf

One of the aspects of Atum.

B

Ba'al

The god of the storm.

Baalat Gebal

A protector goddess.

Babi

The god of virility and representative of male sexuality.

Banebdjedet

Another god of fertility – the ram god.

Ba-Pef

Bringer of spiritual terror.

Bastet

The cat goddess of fertility, protection, fertility, childbirth, and the secrets of women.

Bat

Bringer of fertility and success (also a cat deity).

Bennu

A bird deity associated with Ra, Osiris, and Atum.

Bes

Dwarf god of war, sexuality, childbirth, humor, and fertility.

Beset

Female counterpart of Bes.

Buchis

Depiction of Ka (a bull god).

C

Cavern Deities

They dwelled in the caves under the ground.

Celestial Ferryman

From the underworld, they transported souls across the river boundary.

D

Dedun

Overseer of other gods, offering them protection and resources.

Denwen

Fire deity – often represented by a dragon.

Duamutef

Responsible for the stomach of Horus that was stored in a jar.

E

Ennead

The nine gods of Heliopolis.

F

Fetket

The butler of Ra and also the god of bartenders.

Field of Reeds

Paradise in the afterlife.

Forty-Two Judges

The judges who met with the souls before the heart-weighing ceremony.

Four Sons of Horus

Qebehsenuef, Hapy, Imset, and Duamutef.

G

Geb

God of Earth and the sun of Tefnut and Shu.

Gengen Wer

Around since the beginning of the world – the divine goose.

H

Ha

Protector god of the Western Deserts.

Hapi

The god of fertility and the Nile silt.

Hapy

A protector god and a son of Horus.

Hardedef

King Khufu's son.

Hathor

Among the most significant and popular ancient Egyptian deities. Goddess of war, love, fertility, and the sky.

Hathor-Nebet-Hetepet

The Mother Goddess (Hathor) and the hand of Atum.

Hatmehit

A fish deity associated with rivers and deltas.

Haurun

Is a protector – but also brings death and destruction.

Hedetet

Deity of scorpions and can protect from their sting.

Heh and Hauhet

The frog and serpent deities that represent eternity and infinity.

Heqet

Deity of fertility and birth.

Heret-Kau

Protective goddess who was more powerful than all spirits.

Heka

Primordial form of power and deified form of magic and medicine.

Heryshaf

Ram god of fertility.

Heset

Goddess of food and beverages. She was typically associated with pleasure and beer.

Hetepes-Sekhus

An underworld cobra goddess who was a personification of Ra's eye.

Horus

Avian god that was associated with power, the sky, and the sun.

Hu

The god of the spoken word and the personification of Ra's first word.

I

Iah

A moon god who played an important role in the Egyptian calendar.

Iabet

Deity of fertility and birth.

Ihy

Deity of joy and music.

Imhotep

King Djoser's vizier and the architect of the step pyramid.

Imsety

A protector god and a son of Horus.

Ipy

A Mother Goddess who is associated with Osiris.

Ishtar

Deity of love, sexuality, and war.

Isis

A powerful Egyptian goddess of magic and healing.

Isis-Eutheria

The Greek version of Isis. Her tears formed the Nile river.

Iusaaset

A Mother Goddess and grandmother figure to the other deities.

Iw

A creation deity.

J

Jupiter-Amun

Roman version of Zeus-Amun.

K

Kabechet

Serpent goddess and the daughter of Anubis.

Kagemni

The vizier of King Sneferu – became the god of wisdom after his death.

Kek and Kauket

Gods of night and obscurity.

Khentekhtai

Crocodile god of Lower Egypt's Athribis.

Khentiamentiu

Abydos' god of fertility.

Khenmu

Early Upper Egyptian patron god of potters.

Khepri

An aspect of Ra, who was symbolized by the scarab beetle.

Kherty

Ram-headed god of the Duat, the ancient Egyptian realm of the dead.

Khonsu

A god of the moon who was able to instantly heal the ill.

L

Lady of the Acacia

Grandmother of the deities; another name for Iusaaset. This title was later granted to Hathor.

Lady of the Sycamore

Another name for Hathor.

M

Maahes

Powerful god of the un who protected the innocent.

Maat

The goddess of justice, harmony, and truth. She was among the most significant deities in ancient Egypt.

Mafdet

An early goddess of justice. She declared judgment and was responsible for execution.

Mandulis

Nubian god of the sun – also worshipped in Ancient Egypt.

Mau

The cat of the gods and connected closely to Ra – the cat protected the Tree of Life when it was in danger.

Mehen

Serpent deity and protector of Ra.

Mehet-Weret

The cow deity, and one of the oldest goddesses.

Mehit

An early moon goddess, and is Anhur's consort.

Mekhit

A lioness goddess of war of Nubian origins.

Menhit

The representation of Ra's brow and the lioness and sun goddess.

Meretseger

Cobra deity of protection.

Merit

Musical goddess who could create order.

Meskhenet

Among the oldest ancient Egyptian deities. She was the goddess of childbirth and was thought to attend childbirths. She was responsible for creating the ka and breathing it into the body.

Mestjet

A goddess with the head of a lioness. She was one with the numerous aspects of the Eye of Ra.

Min

The Predynastic Period's god of fertility and the deity of the eastern deserts.

Mnevis

Mnevis was believed to be an aspect of Ra and the divine bull of Heliopolis.

Montu

The falcon god – associated with Horus and Ra.

Mut

This mother goddess played a minor role in early history. However, her significance grew when she later became Amun's wife.

N

Nebethetpet

This goddess was a deification of Atum's hand and was worshiped at Heliopolis.

Nefertum

He was initially one of Atum's aspects but later became known as the god of nice smells and perfume. Nefertum was particularly linked to aromatic flowers.

Nehebkau

This protective god was believed to unite the ka with the ba after an individual died. He was also responsible for uniting the ka with the body at birth.

Nehmetawy

This goddess was worshiped at Hermopolis and was thought to embrace the less fortunate.

Neith

Neith was one of the most popular and lasting ancient Egyptian deities. She was a creator goddess and was linked to Nun. Egyptians believed that she invented birth and was responsible for growth.

Nekhbet

This vulture goddess was linked to Wadjet – often called "The Two Ladies."

Nekheny

Falcon deity that protected.

Neper

The embodiment of corn and the god of grains.

Nephthys

She was among the first five children of Geb and Nut. A goddess of fertility and twin sister of Isis.

Nu and Naunet

The goddess of primordial chaos.

Nut

Wife of Geb and goddess of the primordial sky.

O

Ogdoad

The eight gods of creation: infinity (Heh and Hauhet), water (Nun and Naunet), hiddenness (Amun and Amaunet), and darkness (Kek and Kauket),

Onuris

A god of hunting and war.

Osiris

He was among the first five children of Geb and Nut. Osiris was also the judge of the dead.

P

Pakhet

The lioness goddess of hunting with the vengeful attributes of the goddess Sekmet and the justice and rightfulness of Isis.

Panebtawy

He was the deification of the king. He was Horus' son and represented Horus as a child. He was thought to be the child god.

Peteese and Pihor

Even though they were humans, these brothers were deified due to their link with Osiris. This link was built when they drowned in the Nile River. Ever since then, they have become local protective deities.

Ptah

Ptah was among the oldest ancient Egyptian gods and was believed to be the deity of Memphis, the governor of truth, and the creator of the universe.

Q

Qebehsenuef

Qebehsenuef was one of Horus' sons and was believed to be a protective god in the form of a hawk.

Qudshu

Even though she was a Syrian deity of love, she was worshipped by ancient Egyptian as the goddess of divine ecstasy and sexual pleasure.

R

Ra

The powerful god of the sun of the city of Heliopolis. The pyramids of Giza are linked to this god.

Raettawy

Raettawy was the female aspect of the sun god Ra.

Ra-Harakhte

A god in the form of a falcon that was a blend between Horus and Ra.

Renpet

Renpet was a goddess who deified the year, representing the passage of time.

S

Sah

Sah was an astral god who deified the constellation, Orion. When depicted alongside Sothis, the pair represented Osiris and Isis in their astral forms.

Sekhmet

Sekhmet was among the most important ancient Egyptian deities. She was portrayed as a lion-headed woman and was believed to be the deity of healing and destruction.

Serket

This protective goddess mainly protected against venom. She was also a funerary deity.

Set

The god of chaos, war, and storms.

T

Ta-Bitjet

She was the goddess responsible for safeguarding against venomous and deadly stings. She cast healing spells too.

Tasenetnofret

This protective goddess was a version of Hathor. She was also Horus's companion.

Tatenen

This protective Earth god was related to Ptah.

Taweret

She was the hippopotamus protective goddess of childbirth and fertility. She was also believed to be Bes'consort.

Tayet

She was the weaving Goddess, and she was responsible for supplying clothes and textiles, and mummifications.

Tefnut

The Goddess of moisture and Atum Ra's daughter. She was often portrayed as a lioness or a serpent with the head of a lion.

Tenenit

She was the goddess of beer, brewing, and giving birth.

Thoth

Deity of words, wisdom, and integrity. Some Egyptologists suggest that he was initially a lunar god.

Tjenenyet

This protective goddess was worshiped in Hermonthis. She was also Montu's (the god of war) consort.

Tree Goddesses

The deities associated with trees, such as Hathor, Isis, and Nut.

Triads

A triad is a grouping of 3 significant deities.

Tutu

The god Tutu is known for keeping away from his adversaries and fighting against black magic and demons. He was part human, part snake, part lion, and had wings.

U

Uat-Ur

Deity of the Mediterranean Sea.

Unut

This goddess, with the head of a rabbit and the body of a serpent, was also known as "the rabbit goddess." She was believed to have been an aspect of Ra or Osiris.

W

Wadjet

Daughter of Ra and is a great protective goddess. She appeared in numerous stories about the Eye of Ra, and Weret-Hekau, which means "great magic," was among one of her many names.

Wadj-Wer

Also known as "The Great Green," Wadj-Wer was the deified form of delta lagoons, lakes, and swamps found near the

Mediterranean Sea.

Waset

"The Powerful Female One" was one of Wast's titles. She was known as the city of Thebes' protective goddess.

Weneg

This protective god was closely related to the concept and goddess of Maat. He was believed to keep the peace between the heavens and Earth. He also carried the sky.

Wenenu

He was a hare god and the companion of Wenet, the snake goddess. He was thought to be an aspect of Ra or Osiris.

Wepset

Translates to "She Who Burns." She was known for destroying Osiris' adversaries.

Wepwawet

The name of this god means "Opener of the Ways," alluding to the belief that he cleared the path in wars. He also led the path to life after death, as well as during birth.

Werethekau

The name of this god translates to "Great of Magic." It is a title applied to numerous deities, including Isis and Wadjet.

Y

Yam

Although he was a Phonecian god, Yam made it to the ancient Egyptian pantheon through trade. He also appeared in Egyptian lore because of his battle with Set.

Z

Zenenet

One of the titles given to Isis, Zenenet was particularly used in Hermonthis.

Conclusion

As you have learned from this book, ancient Egyptian magic is one of the oldest known forms of magic. Magic was an essential part of the life of a person from Egypt. It was a fundamental part of medicine and was used by everyone from commoners to officials, royalty, pharaohs, as well as priests, and deities.

Protection magic was used in all elements of a person's life, from warding off evil spirits to curing injuries. The ancient Egyptians even went as far as to use it in rituals meant to ward off invading armies.

Just like in other cultures, in ancient Egypt, magic was either black or white. White magic was good magic that would protect, and black magic was magic that would damage or destroy. White magic could protect babies during birth and mothers during pregnancy; it could promote love or protect those journeying in other worlds.

Heka was the god of magic in ancient Egypt. He was, essentially, the personification of magic, and his name is actually the Egyptian word for magic. Magic was such a fundamental part of ancient Egyptian medicine that physicians were called the "priests of Heka."

Magic permeated every part of ancient Egyptian religious life. One of the primary ancient Egyptian deities, Isis, was one of the strongest magicians in Egypt, and her magical power was said to have been greater than that of the other gods. In fact, it was her magical power that was supposed to protect the kingdom of Egypt from enemies, and she had dominion over fate itself.

Tools used as part of ancient Egyptian magical practice include magic wands, ushabti figures, the sekhem scepter, and the Book of the Dead. However, perhaps the most prominent magical tools used by ancient Egyptians were magical amulets.

Many Egyptian symbols were believed to carry inherent magical power, and these symbols were made into amulets that were carried by individuals and placed with the dead in their tombs. Some well-known symbols and amulets include the ankh, the scarab, and the Wedjat eye. Other types of ancient Egyptian magic include divination and plant magic.

Over the years, ancient Egyptian magic and religion have been used in a variety of esoteric beliefs and societies, such as by the Hermetic Order of the Golden Dawn. However, despite these variations, it is still possible to find the history of true ancient Egyptian magic and religion – and this book has helped you to do exactly that.

Here's another book by Mari Silva that you might like

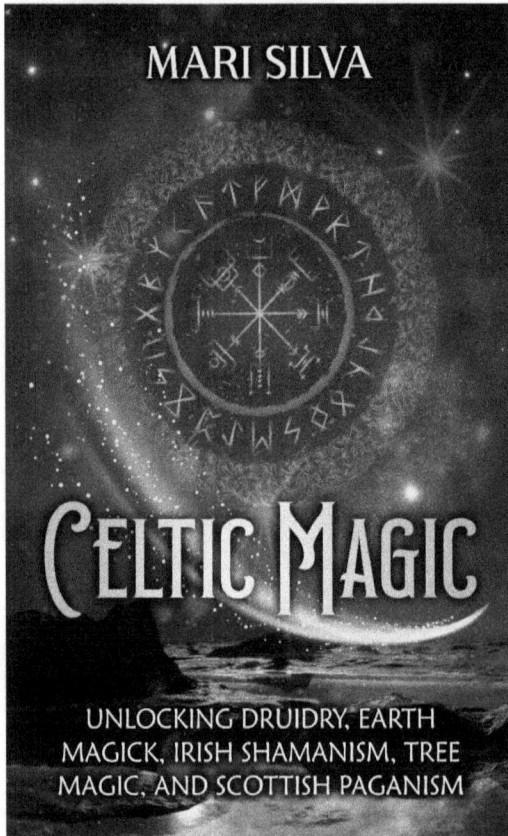

MARI SILVA

CELTIC MAGIC

UNLOCKING DRUIDRY, EARTH
MAGICK, IRISH SHAMANISM, TREE
MAGIC, AND SCOTTISH PAGANISM

Your Free Gift
(only available for a limited time)

Thanks for getting this book! If you want to learn more about various spirituality topics, then join Mari Silva's community and get a free guided meditation MP3 for awakening your third eye. This guided meditation mp3 is designed to open and strengthen ones third eye so you can experience a higher state of consciousness. Simply visit the link below the image to get started.

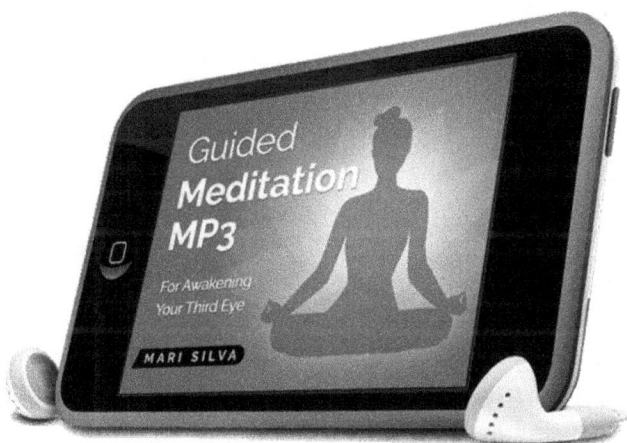

https://spiritualityspot.com/meditation

References

Ellison, T. (2021, June 15). Magic in the ancient world: Egyptian deities and uses. TheCollector. https://www.thecollector.com/magic-ancient-world-egyptian-deities/

Harris, E. (2016). Ancient Egyptian magic. Red Wheel/Weiser.

Mark, J. J. (2017). Magic in ancient Egypt. World History Encyclopedia. https://www.worldhistory.org/article/1019/magic-in-ancient-egypt/

Egyptian civilization - Myths - Creation myth. (n.d.). Historymuseum.Ca. https://www.historymuseum.ca/cmc/exhibitions/civil/egypt/egcr09e.html

McLean, J. (n.d.). Ancient Egyptian religion. Lumenlearning.com https://courses.lumenlearning.com/suny-hccc-worldcivilization/chapter/ancient-egyptian-religion/

San-Aset. (2020, July 13). The seven principles of ma'at. Iseum Sanctuary. https://iseumsanctuary.com/2020/07/12/the-seven-principles-of-maat/

Themes, W. (2019, June 11). The Egyptian ceremony of the weighing of the heart. St James Ancient Art. https://www.ancient-art.co.uk/the-egyptian-cerimony-of-the-the-weighing-of-the-heart/

Alvar, J. (2020, March 22). *Worship of this Egyptian goddess spread from Egypt to England.* National Geographic. https://www.nationalgeographic.co.uk/history-and-civilisation/2020/03/worship-of-this-egyptian-goddess-spread-from-egypt-to-england

Apep (apophis). (n.d.). Ancientegyptonline.co.uk. https://ancientegyptonline.co.uk/apep/

Bastet (bast). (n.d.-a). Egyptianmuseum.org https://egyptianmuseum.org/deities-Bastet

Bastet (bast). (n.d.-b). Egyptianmuseum.org
https://egyptianmuseum.org/deities-Bastet

Bastet (bast). (n.d.-c). Egyptianmuseum.org.
https://egyptianmuseum.org/deities-Bastet

Caro, T. (2021, January 7). How to Know if a Goddess is Calling you? [Signs Explained]. *Magickal Spot.* https://magickalspot.com/is-goddess-calling-me/

Category:Maat-goddess (hieroglyph). (n.d.). Wikimedia.org.
https://commons.wikimedia.org/wiki/Category:Maat-goddess_(hieroglyph)

Connecting with Neith? (n.d.). Reddit.
https://www.reddit.com/r/witchcraft/comments/p2sjed/connecting_with_neith/

Cult of Isis. (n.d.). Wabash.edu
http://persweb.wabash.edu/facstaff/royaltyr/AncientCities/web/rel%20372%20project/ISIS.htm

Deprez, G. (2021, April 24). *Goddess Isis: Fascinating facts about the mother of all gods.* TheCollector. https://www.thecollector.com/ancient-egyptian-goddess-isis/

Egyptian civilization - Myths - The divine family. (n.d.). Historymuseum.Ca.
https://www.historymuseum.ca/cmc/exhibitions/civil/egypt/egcr10e.html

Explore deities in ancient Egypt. (n.d.). Egyptianmuseum.org.
https://egyptianmuseum.org/deities-overview

Fields, K. (2020, February 18). *Bastet: 9 ways to work with the Egyptian cat goddess of the home.* Otherworldly Oracle; FIELDS CREATIVE CONSULTING. https://otherworldlyoracle.com/bastet-egyptian-cat-goddess/

Fields, K. (2022, June 26). *Isis Goddess of Magic: 12 ways to work with her POWERFUL energy.* Otherworldly Oracle; FIELDS CREATIVE CONSULTING. https://otherworldlyoracle.com/isis-goddess/

Fulton, N. (2020). *Serqet: A bug, a brother, and a great big bomb.* Independently Published.

Geller. (2016, October 17). *Neith.* Mythology.net.
https://mythology.net/egyptian/egyptian-gods/neith/

Gerges, F. A. (2021). *ISIS: A History.* Princeton University Press.

Hill, B. (2019, June 9). *Maat: Ancient Egyptian goddess of truth, justice and morality.* Ancient Origins. https://www.ancient-origins.net/history-ancient-traditions/maat-ancient-egyptian-goddess-truth-justice-and-morality-003131

Isis: Goddess symbols, correspondences, myth & offerings. (2021, July 2).
Spells8. https://spells8.com/lessons/isis-goddess-worship/

Jay, N. (2020, December 1). *Neith – creator of the universe.* Symbol Sage.

https://symbolsage.com/neith-egyptian-goddess/

Lesso, R. (2022, May 31). *Why was sekhmet important to ancient Egyptians?* TheCollector. https://www.thecollector.com/why-was-sekhmet-important-to-ancient-egyptians/

LibGuides: Bastet: About. (2021a). https://westportlibrary.libguides.com/bastet

LibGuides: Bastet: About. (2021b). https://westportlibrary.libguides.com/bastet

Maat. (n.d.). The Fitzwilliam Museum. https://fitzmuseum.cam.ac.uk/objects-and-artworks/highlights/context/tradition-and-change/maat

Ma'at. (n.d.). Enlightenment Through Hellfire https://scarletarosa.tumblr.com/post/631441701809029120/maat-egyptian-goddess-of-truth-justice-harmony

Maat - Egyptian Goddess of Justice. (2013, April 3). Crystal Vaults. https://www.crystalvaults.com/goddess-maat/

Maat symbol. (2018, July 2). Ancient Symbols. https://www.ancient-symbols.com/symbols-directory/maat.html